RISE. ALIGN. *Shine.*

Living Boldly in Faith, Purpose and Joy

MICHELE GUNN

ISBN: 978-1-971349-19-0

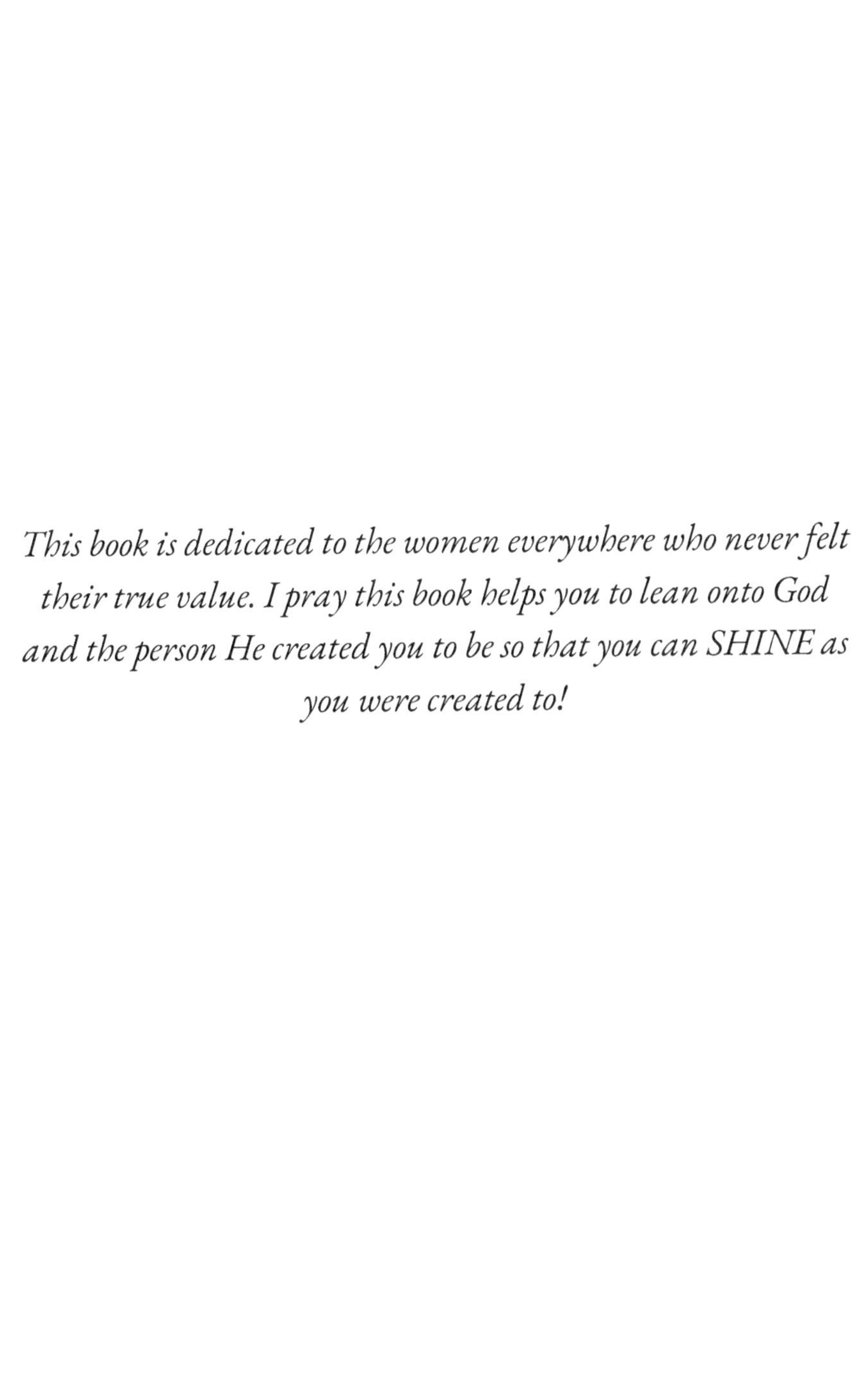

This book is dedicated to the women everywhere who never felt their true value. I pray this book helps you to lean onto God and the person He created you to be so that you can SHINE as you were created to!

Acknowledgements

Before anything else, I give thanks to God, who called me long before I understood the call. This book exists because He gently and persistently invited me to trust Him, to grow, and to step forward in faith. When I doubted myself, He reminded me who He created me to be. When I hesitated, He equipped me. When I questioned timing, He reassured me that His timing is perfect. As Scripture reminds us:

"Before I formed you in the womb I knew you, before you were born I dedicated you, a prophet to the nations I appointed you." —Jeremiah 1:5

I carry these words close to my heart, knowing that this work is not mine alone, but part of something God began long before I ever picked up a pen.

To my husband, Gary, thank you for your continued love, patience, support, and encouragement. You have walked beside me through every season; celebrating the victories, steadying me in the doubts, and believing in me even when I struggled to believe in myself. Your presence has been a constant reminder that I do not walk this journey of life alone.

To my children, Amanda, Matthew, and Keri, thank you for your support, your encouragement, and for unknowingly giving me so much material to write about. You have been my teachers, my inspiration, and my reminder of what truly matters. Watching you grow has shaped my faith, deepened my purpose, and strengthened my desire to live boldly and authentically.

I am deeply grateful to Fr. Tom Ponzini, whose spiritual example continues to inspire me. Your life reflects what it means to be a giver, to serve selflessly, and to live faith in action. Thank you for your encouragement and support along this journey.

To Vic Clesceri, thank you for always pulling me back to faith and for teaching me what it means to surrender. Your wisdom, perspective, and unwavering trust in God have been a grounding force and a gentle reminder to let go and let God lead.

My sincere thanks to the She Rises Studios publishing team for your knowledge, professionalism, encouragement, and belief in this message. Your support throughout this process has been invaluable, and I am grateful for the care and excellence you brought to this book.

To the women in my life (family, friends, mentors, prayer warriors, and fellow pilgrims) thank you for standing with me, lifting me up, and reminding me of my purpose when I needed it most. Your support has been a gift beyond words.

Finally, to the readers of *Graceful Awakening*, thank you for walking with me, supporting this calling, and allowing me to live out my purpose through writing. Your openness, encouragement, and shared faith make this work meaningful and alive.

May this book meet you where you are, encourage you to rise in faith, align your life with God's purpose, and shine boldly in the joy you were created to live.

Table of Contents

Acknowledgements 5

Introduction 9

Rise: Awakening Faith & Identity 11

My Story 13

Who Are You 22

Forgiveness 29

The RISE Framework...36

Facing Fear and Overcoming Self 42

Align: Living in Harmony with God's Design 49

Speaking Life 51

The Whole Wellbeing (Mind, Body, Spirit)..........................63

Let's Talk About Growth (and Seasons of Life) 74

Finding Purpose as the Key to Joy 85

What is Success? 97

Shine: Impact, Legacy & Living Boldly 103

Community, Relationships & Service.....................................105

Leaving a Legacy 111

Legacy Action Plan 115

Empowerment to Live It Out 119

Now Go! 125

About the Author..127

Introduction:
An invitation to begin the journey of living boldly in faith, purpose, and joy.

Since I started to feel the tug of faith, I have felt drawn toward Matthew 28:19-20, "Go, therefore, and make disciples of all nations, baptizing them in the name of the Father, and of the Son, and of the holy Spirit, teaching them to observe all that I have commanded you. And behold, I am with you always, until the end of the age." For years, I wrestled with what this scripture truly meant for my life. Over time, God revealed that it wasn't just a command for the Church. It was a call for me, personally.

As I have found myself and embraced my God-given talents during my lifelong journey, I am finding my true purpose. That purpose is helping women awaken their faith, align their lives, and shine with purpose. I believe you, too, are called to something more. This book is an invitation for you to discover the freedom and confidence that come when your faith, life, and purpose align with God's design.

My prayer is that these pages help you to break free from fear, self-doubt, and comparison. I also pray that you will begin your journey to discover your God-given identity and strengths. You will also learn how to cultivate forgiveness and speak life through faith-filled affirmations, embrace your wholeness (mind, body, and spirit) and to step boldly into your calling to shine Christ's light into the world.

This isn't just a book to read, it's a journey to live. Think of it as walking a path where each chapter is a step that brings you closer to God's heart and your truest self. Woven throughout are reflection questions and action steps to guide you on your journey. Each chapter also ends with ***Walking with God*** to help you deepen your relationship with Him. Take your time and do the work. Revisit chapters as needed. You don't have to keep blending into the background. The time has come to rise with courage, align with God's truth, and shine with joy and purpose.

Now, find a quiet spot to take this book to then open your heart and begin your journey.

Reflection

- Where do you feel God tugging at your heart right now?
- How do you see yourself in Matthew 28:19–20?
- Is God calling you to something more?
- What fears or comparisons do you need to let go of in order to rise into your true identity?

Prayer

Heavenly Father, thank You for inviting me into this journey. Open my heart as I begin these pages. Show me who I am in You. Help me to release fear and doubt, and give me courage to rise, align, and shine with the purpose You have placed within me. Speak to me through Your Word, and let Your Spirit guide me every step of the way. Amen.

Author's Note: *All Scripture quotations in this book are taken directly from the United States Conference of Catholic Bishops (USCCB) online Bible (www.usccb.org). I chose this source because it is Catholic, faithful to the text, and allows God's Word to speak for itself.*

RISE:
AWAKENING FAITH & IDENTITY

My Story:
How God shaped my journey and how He can transform yours.

"They conquered him by the blood of the Lamb and by the word of their testimony; love for life did not deter them from death."
—Revelation 12:11

I never dreamed of becoming a writer, or even writing. I have lived a rather mundane and ordinary life. Don't get me wrong, I have accomplishments. One of the things I am most proud of is my children. I have contributed to society by the work I produced and the humans I created. I have always longed for more. My story is not extraordinary. It is filled with uncertainties, self-doubt and struggle. Even as a life coach, I still struggle with self-confidence. I have not reached some millionaire success ending that you hear and read about people doing. They become this huge success by reaching some determined monetary number and will sell you their secret! Most people live in the ordinary. That does not mean they never reach success. I see success as defined in the ordinary.

I was born in Michigan and grew up in a family of seven on an Arabian horse farm. I was the middle of five children, being the oldest of the second set (at least it felt that way). My father worked at least 40 hours a week and then came home and worked the farm. He also worked the farm on weekends. My mother took care of five kids ranging 12 years apart from youngest to oldest. Four girls and one boy. She also managed the horse farm; breeding, raising, training, showing and selling horses.

We lived a modest life of simplicity, but never truly lacked for basic needs. The oldest three kids had plenty of chores as the horse business was the priority of time and money. We all learned how to do farm chores; feeding animals, cleaning stalls, baling hay, driving tractor, etc. The older daughters did the majority of household chores. Overall, it was a good life in a small rural town. But something was missing, at least for me. I never felt like I belonged.

The farm totaled about 20 acres. One thing I learned from farm life is that it wasn't for me. I suffered from allergies and learned just how much during hay season. Sure, I rode horses and enjoyed the outdoors, but I was far from outdoorsy and preferred to be inside. Back then, I had no idea who I was or what my strengths were. I was encouraged to do as I was told and I did.

I was a meek child, although I don't remember most of my childhood. We attended church every week, seasonally. After all, in the horse business, attending horse shows was a must. The horse business determined our family schedule, expenditures...well, life. I was never encouraged to chase interests. I loved the piano. My mom loved the organ, so I took organ lessons. As a young child I dreamt of working in an office, possibly becoming a lawyer.

My maternal grandparents, whom we were very involved with, were faithfully religious people. Remember, we attended church regularly when there were no horse shows. We attended faith formation classes in the next town where our church was located, until our school created a new schedule that clashed with the faith formation class schedule. We just got home too late from school to make it there on time. I was not really encouraged to grow in faith or to know God.

As a child, I did well in school. I was not a perfect student, but got good grades. I remember in first grade, my teacher put tape on my mouth for talking too much. That would not be tolerated today. Also, knowing what I know now, that was a sign of one of my strengths (gift). All through school, I remember doing well, not at the top of the class, but the top 25%. I was in the National Honor Society in high school. I do remember having difficulties in math (and maybe more) in the 6th grade. I don't remember why or what happened, but surely I was a disappointment to my parents. After all, they parented like most, pointing out what was wrong and glossing over what was right and good. I was expected to get good grades. Period.

While growing up, I remember feeling unloved. Unloved by my parents, grandparents and siblings. I had no self-value. Attention was given to those involved in horses. Each child was treated differently. Having three children of my own, I understand that, but I sure hope none of my kids ever felt unloved! Of course looking back, I know what I would do differently to encourage each one of my children to excel in their God-given gifts. We can't go back, so I focus on the present.

In my early teen years, change started. At least that is how I remember it. I had such low self-esteem. I felt so unloved. I knew deep down that I was the one who could change it. That is when I started self-affirmations. I never heard of that before, but that is what I did. Every morning, I looked at myself in the mirror and told myself I was pretty, I was smart, I was lovable and more. I don't really remember the exact words that I told myself, but I continued affirming myself with compliments until I believed them. I still continue and watch my self-value grow!

Entering high school, I felt (no, I knew!) that my parents had certain expectations of me. Let's be honest. These expectations showed in their actions as well as in their words. They pushed me to excel in school (beyond my own self-conceived limits). I was required to take all of the advanced classes, no matter how hard they were and how much I struggled. I remember staying after math class every day in my Senior year because I just didn't get it. I witnessed other kids receive support from their parents to follow the path they had passion for. I was pushed for a path that had the potential to create financial stability. Even then, I was not about the money. I wanted happiness. No. I wanted JOY.

My parents wanted me to be an engineer. To this day, I am so glad I did not follow their path for me. Reading over college course guide books, I discovered MARKETING! That sounded like something I could really enjoy!! Since it was a business degree, I was permitted to pursue it. I was blessed that my parents paid for almost all of my college. With that, comes control. Control over me that I had felt my entire life thus far. I was accepted to the University of Michigan!! GO BLUE!! I was permitted to attend the University of Michigan-Flint. I could commute there. I could work 30 hours a week while taking a full college course load, driving 45 minutes to and 45 minutes from school. I was not permitted to join clubs, hang out or network. Knowing now who I am, this stunted my growth in my strengths (gifts).

During my last year of college, I met my husband. Life plans changed. We wanted a family so we decided to put my career on hold. I would be a stay-at-home mom. This was the most important thing I could do with my life. When I became pregnant, my husband was excited to share the news. Me, I was frightened. I would be yet another disappointment because as the first college graduate in my family, I chose to not begin a career, but to begin a family and raise our children. Fortunately, my parents were thrilled about having their first grandchild. We ended up with three beautiful children.

This is when my path of faith truly began to build on the light foundation I already had. With babies and faith comes Baptism. We needed a church. We needed to belong if we would grow our faith-filled family. Did I mention that I am Catholic and my husband is Baptist? Yup. Things not discussed before marriage because neither one was involved with church, but we both believed in and loved God. There would be challenges ahead.

As our kids were growing up in our one income household, we had financial challenges. Remember, I was not about the money. Actually, I had money issues and so did my husband. We were opposites. He enjoyed spending freely and I was so afraid we would end up with nothing, that I couldn't spend money unless it was for a necessity. He worked in a trade linked to the auto industry, so there were ups and downs. We both agreed to raise our kids in the Catholic faith. They needed to attend Faith Formation classes. They gave teachers a discount so I volunteered to teach. You have to know the subject to teach it so I began learning with my children.

It wasn't until we ended up moving when our kids were in elementary and middle school that I took a full time job at a church for a little extra money. It gave me something to do and I was still able to be there for my family. This is where we all grew spiritually. This is where we found home. This church, and the people in it, became our family. My eagerness to teach my husband about the Catholic faith had me asking questions so I could answer him. When I asked the office manager questions, she told me where to find the answer. Hmmm....teaching a (wo)man to fish.

The more I learned and got involved, the more I felt alive. Prayer groups, social activities, marketing for the Catholic school... WAIT!! Did you know that evangelization is essentially marketing Jesus?? Matthew 28:19 has always been a favorite Bible verse of mine: "Go, therefore, and make disciples of all nations, baptizing them in the name of the Father, and of the Son, and of the holy Spirit," Part of the inner me started to blossom as I began to align (unknowingly) my innate talents to who I am. I was learning who God created me to be.

We were very happy in our life. Then the auto industry crashed in Michigan. My husband lost his job and I was making very little. Oh, we had also just registered two kids for Catholic School!! God, family and our church family helped us to get them though that year! Unemployment offered hardship and opportunity. Opportunity presented itself when my husband had time to visit with the priest often. This led to him converting to Catholicism at the same Mass that my two oldest children were Confirmed in the faith. Opportunity was presented when we were all in the car together praying the Rosary. That did not happen before, because we didn't have as much time together.

My husband's unemployment brought us closer together, closer to God and taught us how to allow other people to be a blessing in our lives. As people, we often want credit for helping other people. We do not want to be the ones needing help. It was told to me to allow people to help. It would allow me to bless them by allowing them to bless our family. This is something I still teach often today.

We finally got to a point that we knew we needed to move out of state so my husband could gain better employment. We decided on Texas. My youngest sister and her family would be moving there, so we thought that could be a bonus with the thriving economy. My husband contacted a recruiter who set up interviews. We packed up a car and sent my husband to Texas to start our new life. The kids and I would move after the school year ended.

Before my husband left for Texas, I was gifted a spot at a weekend silent retreat. I did not think I was capable of being silent that long! This was a time when I was able to make a stronger connection with Father, Son and Holy Spirit! Time in nature, time spent reading the Bible, time spent in prayer and time spent listening to God all prepared me for the next steps in my lifelong journey. It was definitely time I needed with God.

I thought since the kids were older, I would start my marketing career. I did marketing part time for the Catholic school back home, so I had some experience. I can only assume that my age and lack of experience was not the combination potential employers were looking for. Interviews went well, but I never got an offer of employment. I decided to look in the field of my last job, the church. I started in Internal Audit and ended up managing a large country church where I found my passion.

Looking back, I know God had a plan for me. There were clues along the way that I either ignored or just didn't see. I received a message (that I always held in my mind and heart) from a prayer team member, the marketing degree (how to evangelize), the family life, the struggles, the church work (I did work elsewhere, too, but that is another story) and the growing in faith. It was at the last church where the pastor and I both wanted more for our parishioners. We wanted them to find purpose in their church work, as well as in themselves, so I was tasked with finding a way to do that. That is how I came across CliftonStengths®. My pastor agreed that it would be great to implement at the church. We weighed our options. It was less expensive to have someone trained in-house to do the work. I felt a pull to become a Gallup Certified Strengths Coach to serve our parish. The pastor agreed. I believe he saw in me what I had yet to find.

When I took the CliftonStrengths® assessment and received my results, I was not surprised. Well, a couple things surprised me, but after I learned more, it became clear who I am and who I was meant to be. I understood why faith was my foundation and why I had skills to accomplish things that did not bring me joy. With the blessing of my pastor, I founded Cultivate and Thrive. I am a Coach. Specifically, a Self-actualization and Mindset Coach. My mission is to live out my Christian faith by embracing the interconnectedness of all things and recognizing that every individual is of inherent value and importance. I am committed to helping people (specifically women) discover their worth, empowering them to realize their potential, and making a positive impact in their lives. Through acts of compassion, service, and love, I aim to spread kindness, inspire hope, and foster a sense of belonging within my community and beyond. By living authentically, guided by my spiritual beliefs, I strive to be a beacon of light, encouraging others to embrace their own unique journey with faith, grace and purpose.

Success to me is defined as helping at least one person realize their value and use that value to help others. I am happy to be used as God's instrument over and over to reach success one person at a time.

My prayer is to empower you to embrace your unique, God-given talents through a story of faith and finding purpose. I want you to know that there is not an expiration date on success and the world needs the person you are created to be.

The common thread in my ordinary story is FAITH. As my faith grew, my self-value grew. God provided opportunities for me to grow in confidence and strength. He provided direction (although at times I got lost) to help me find my purpose. God has always placed people in my life to help guide me and bring me back to Him when I went astray. I hope and pray this book provides strength, directions, encouragement, motivation and tools to help you start on a path to discover and embrace who God created you to be.

I did not read a lot of books to enlighten me or change my thinking about who I am or how I should be. I have read a few that have enlightened me to open my heart and my mind to who God created me to be. I have participated in a few book discussions, meeting weekly, to share learnings and talk about how different people interpreted the meanings of each line or topic in the book. These books did not define me or change me. They enlightened me, educated me and opened my mind. God has spoken through some of them.

That said, I don't expect this book to change you. You do need to do the work. Use this book as a guide, a journal and a chance to get to know **YOU**! Questions have been provided so you can start your own journey of discovery. Space has been provided to jot down first thoughts. Listen as God speaks to you, through you.

Reflection

- How does hearing someone else's testimony encourage your own walk of faith?
- What moments in your life could be part of your testimony?
- Who might be waiting to hear your story?

Prayer

Lord, thank You for working in my life through every season. Help me see how my story can bring hope and encouragement to others. Amen.

Walking with God

Have you talked to God about your story? How would He describe your story? Knowing that He created you with love, knowing that he has gifted you with unique talents and knowing He has plans for you; how do you envision that conversation? Picture it. Take time and sit somewhere quiet. Invite God to join you. Start the conversation.

Who Are You:
Discovering your true identity as God's beloved child.

"But you are a chosen race, a royal priesthood, a holy nation, a people of his own, so that you may announce the praises' of him who called you out of darkness into his wonderful light."
—1 Peter 2:9

Many times we are told who we are and who we should be. This usually begins with our parents. There is usually no ill intention, it is just what parents are taught and then they repeat it with their own children. Most of us were not taught to look at a child and see what is right with them. We look to see what is wrong or what needs to be fixed. We ask, "Is the child progressing physically, emotionally and mentally at average levels?" " What can we do to get them to be above average?" We strive for our kids to be above average. We do forget that most people will not be above average. After all, when referring to people, average means what is expected or typical. Everyone cannot be "above average," but everyone can be uniquely gifted.

Then there is the idea of the well-rounded person. I know when I attended college in the 80s, we needed to have classes that had nothing to do with our major, but they were supposed to make us a well-rounded person. It is common knowledge that the majority of people will not be good at a large variety of things. We each have our own special skills and talents. As children, our God-given (innate) talents are more easily seen.

These talents are usually raw, meaning they need to be developed. Talents at the raw stage can often appear to be weaknesses. For example, a child who talks a lot in class and even in general can be seen as a child who needs to learn to be quiet. They are often stifled much like I was as a child. In reality, this is a talent related to communication and relationship building. When properly nurtured and invested in, this talent can be used for many successful outcomes like team building, writing, and public speaking. A child that asks a lot of questions can be seen as bothersome. In reality, they have an inquisitive mind that searches for information. This can still seem annoying when an adult exhibits that behavior, but in reality it is a strength. Searching for information helps to create the best solutions. If this is stifled, we could lose important inventors or problem solvers.

We are also taught to overlook certain strengths in a person. If their strength does not fit into what we see as ideal or what we need, we tend to ignore it. Artistic kids are often encouraged to be more academic, especially if they show skills in other areas. We work hard to get the kid to fit the mold. If a kid daydreams a lot, it is stifled. We tell them they need to live in reality. These dreamers are often inventors, story writers and idea makers. Kids who are quiet and spend time thinking alone are encouraged to be more social and to spend time in the present. Again, this is a strength that should be nurtured. I am not saying that we should ignore areas that often need improvement. I am saying we should feed areas of natural ability.

As we get older, most often this encouragement to fit the mold is even more drastic. Socially, we need to fit in. Professionally, we need to reach certain levels of a defined success. Performance reviews are written and given to encourage and reward people to be a certain way. At a church where I was the business administrator, I proposed a new annual review process. The pastor approved it. Since we had all staff take the CliftonStrengths® assessment, I created an evaluation for them to complete based on their strengths. Having each employee review and answer the questions to then discuss with the pastor, helped keep them highly engaged in their roles. It also helped to ensure that they were able to use their talents to give the best of who they are. It also provided opportunities for them to ask for what they needed to fit their definition of success. It was a very positive experience.

So now it is time to think about who you are and who you were created to be. You need to reflect on who you were as a child as well as who you are now. Prayerfully answer the questions that follow. It is important to be honest with yourself. Share what first comes to mind and share what you think after some deep contemplation.

As a child, what qualities did people comment on the most (positive and negative comments)?

____

____

____

____

As a teenager, what qualities did people comment on the most (positive and negative comments)?

____

____

____

____

As an adult, what qualities do people comment on the most (positive and negative comments)?

____

____

____

____

Where have you seen success in your life?

____

____

____

____

What are your greatest dreams (dream big!)?

____

____

____

____

What things come easy to you and bring joy?

____

____

What parts of you (talents/skills) are you eager to share with others?

____

____

____

____

What do people come to you for?

____

____

____

____

What values do you hold?

____

____

____

____

What are your beliefs (faith, work, relationships, ethics)?

____

____

____

____

How do you joyfully serve others in everyday life?

____

____

____

____

Reflect on these questions and the answer you provided. These questions and answers are tools to get to know yourself better. If you are unsure, or even for added analysis, ask a friend, coworker or family member to answer the relevant questions about you. Look for patterns in behavior and patterns in responses. Oftentimes, you can complete an assessment that will help guide you and offer confirmation of who you are. My favorite is the CliftonStrengths® Talent assessment. Being a Gallup Certified Strengths Coach, I truly understand the value this assessment provides. It offers insight into who you innately are as well as confirmation or affirmation of who you know you are!

<u>*Reflection*</u>

- What words or labels do you most often use to describe yourself?
- How do these align (or conflict) with how God describes you?
- What would it mean for you to fully live as "chosen and beloved"?

<u>*Prayer*</u>

Father, remind me daily that I am Your child. Strip away false identities and help me walk boldly in who You created me to be. Amen.

<u>*Walking with God*</u>

Spend time with Jesus. Ask Him the questions in this chapter, rephrasing them to get His view of you. Really picture the interaction in your mind. Listen intently. What is He saying to you? What memories does He talk about? What does He love most about you? Ask Him if He sees Himself in you.

Forgiveness: Breaking Free from the Chains of the Past to Rise Renewed.

Many of us struggle internally with things that have happened to us or with things we have done. We often cannot get beyond where we believe we have fallen short to move forward. We may have hurt others or we may have hurt ourselves. Some things may be small. Some things may be large, or they may just **FEEL** large. There are often reminders of our failures or wrong doings. Sometimes we are even reminded every day.

The raw truth is: if you do not value yourself, who can value you? This is where forgiveness comes in. You need to forgive yourself so you can value yourself! You need to forgive yourself so you can move forward!

Pray 2 CORINTHIANS 5:17, "So whoever is in Christ is a new creation: the old things have passed away; behold, new things have come."

Practice **FORGIVE**: Find, Own, Realize, Give, Internalize, Vindicate, Embrace.

Find: Spend time thinking about things that may have happened or you may have done that don't feel right.

Own: Own your behaviors or events that happened.

__Realize:__ Realize that these things do NOT define you.

__Give:__ Give love, support and kindness to others and yourself.

__Internalize:__ Feel the love and support within. Start with gratitude and feel peace.

__Vindicate:__ Set yourself free from these things that you found and owned.

__Embrace:__ Embrace you. Love you. Know your value.

Holding on to hurt, disappointment, wrong-doing, etc. will only cause you to suffer and to be stuck. Remember that you may be flawed, but you are still fabulous! Let's consider the concept of being beautifully flawed, as designed by God, and how imperfections can be seen as strengths in disguise. God created us to need one another. We were not meant to live life alone. He has given us differing strengths just as 1 Corinthians 12:12 states, "As a body is one though it has many parts, and all the parts of the body, though many, are one body, so also Christ." One part is just one part, but many parts make a whole.

From a faith-based perspective, we need to embrace our flaws as part of God's plan for personal growth. He provides people in our life or people to cross our path to help us grow and work together. We have opportunities to see the gifts in others so that we can work together while lifting each other up.

Who has God put in your life to help you?

____

____

____

How have their gifts impacted your life?

____

____

____

Knowing that you were never intended to be perfect, frees us from that burden. It provides us an opportunity to embrace all we were created to be.

Utilize this short program to help heal yourself. Remember, we are all unique individuals with innate talents and strengths that provide value that others need. Let's FORGIVE ourselves and others.

Forgive Yourself

Use this to help you work through anything you need to forgive yourself for:

Find: Spend time thinking about things that may have happened or you may have done that don't feel right. Write them down. There is something freeing about getting it out of your mind and on to paper.

____

____

____

____

____

Own: Own your behaviors or events that happened. Accept what you did or what happened. Accept your reactions. Own your behaviors and your feelings. Remember that just because it ***was*** you, it doesn't mean it still has to ***be*** you. Owning means taking accountability. How will you ***own*** these things or events?

____

____

____

____

Realize: Realize that these things do **NOT** define you. You were created with innate talents and gifts. You were also created with Free Will. A bad decision or bad action does not define you. How you grow, become a better person and give to others will define you. You cannot erase the past, but you can build upon it with improvements to create a better you for the future. How will you grow and improve from past mistakes?

____

____

____

____

Give: Give love, support and kindness to others and yourself. I have been a longtime believer and supporter of giving without expectation of receiving. It seems our world teaches us to only give when you will receive something. Even fundraising for great causes offers t-shirts, book bags, magnets, etc. Churches offer your name on a plaque. That sure is sad. I read a book recommended by a friend called "The Go-Giver: A Little Story About a Powerful Business Idea" by John David Mann and Bob Burg. It is more than a powerful business idea, it should be a personal mission. How will you give to yourself and others?

____

____

____

____

Internalize: Feel the love and support within. Start with gratitude and feel peace. You need to feel the positivity. There is absolutely nothing wrong with it. In fact, as God's creation, you should love yourself. That doesn't mean you need to be boastful or have a huge ego, but you do need to love yourself. What is lovable about you? Name some great reasons/qualities below.

____

____

____

____

Vindicate: Set yourself free from these things that you found and owned. You can even go to Confession to help you set those things free. If there are people you need to apologize to, do it. Don't forget to apologize to yourself for holding things against you. Do it out loud and in front of a mirror. Look yourself in the eyes. Feel it. Accept it. Feel it leave you. What do you need forgiveness for?

____

____

____

____

Embrace: Embrace you. Love you. Know your value. Do the work to know who you are and to forgive yourself for anything you need to. What do you embrace about yourself? What do you still need to work on?

____

____

____

____

True forgiveness takes work, hard work. It can be more difficult to forgive yourself than to forgive others. Remember Matthew 18:22, "Jesus answered, 'I say to you, not seven times but seventy-seven times'." We are called to forgive. Do the work. It will make a difference in how you view others as well as how you view yourself.

Reflection

- Who in your life do you need to forgive?
- What's holding you back from forgiving yourself?

- How might forgiveness free you to rise higher in faith?

Prayer

Jesus, teach me to forgive as You have forgiven me. Heal my heart and release me from bitterness, shame, and regret. Amen.

Walking with God

This is it! This is your time to have that conversation with God. Find a quiet place. Center your heart and mind. Ask Jesus to come talk with you. You have something important to share. Jesus is here for you. He is waiting for you to open up with honesty and vulnerability. Tell Jesus what you need forgiveness for. Ask for His forgiveness. Hear His forgiveness. Also ask Jesus to help you give forgiveness to others where it has been difficult to forgive. Feel Him put His arm around you as you talk and He offers you strength and wisdom. Feel the love, acceptance and strength.

The RISE Framework:
A practical model for stepping into God's design with courage and hope.

"Arise! Shine, for your light has come, the glory of the LORD has dawned upon you."
—Isaiah 60:1

Years ago, I created a post on LinkedIn. Without realizing it, it became a life principle: RISE — Realize, Individual, Significance, Everywhere. I am all about lifting people up and valuing people for who they are. So, it wasn't just an acronym. It was a challenge, a reminder, and a truth I needed to hold onto. At the time, I was learning to see myself through God's eyes not just as a woman with a list of things to do, roles to fulfill and responsibilities to carry, but as His unique creation with a purpose that went beyond titles, circumstances, or seasons of life.

RISE became a compass, pointing me toward living fully awake to the value God placed within me. And it's a compass I now offer to you.

R – Realize

Realizing is more than knowing, it's awakening. It's that moment when the truth you've heard a hundred times finally settles deep into your soul: I am valuable. I am called. I am loved.

So many of us walk through life on autopilot, unaware of the extraordinary gifts God has woven into our being. We dismiss compliments, minimize our talents, and overlook the ways we impact others. Scripture reminds us:

"May the eyes of [your] hearts be enlightened, that you may know what is the hope that belongs to his call, what are the riches of glory in his inheritance among the holy ones," (Ephesians 1:18) Realizing your worth is the first step toward living it. You can't live out what you haven't yet recognized and what you haven't yet embraced.

Reflection: What is one truth about who you are in Jesus that you need to really believe today?

____

____

I – Individual

God did not create you as a duplicate. You are an original who is crafted intentionally, intricately, and intimately. Psalm 139:14 says, "I praise you, because I am wonderfully made; wonderful are your works! My very self you know." That means your quirks, your strengths, your flaws, your life experiences (yes, even the challenging ones) are part of your intentional design. In my work as a Gallup Certified CliftonStrengths® coach, I've seen this over and over: when people lean into their God-given strengths, they flourish. They stop trying to be who the world says they should be and start embracing who God made them to be.

Reflection: Write down three things that make you uniquely you. Thank God for each one.

____

____

S – Significance

Significance is different from success. Success can be fleeting, dependent on achievements, recognition, or external validation. Significance is rooted in purpose and impact, it's eternal. Jesus reminds us in John 15:16: "It was not you who chose me, but I who chose you and appointed you to go and bear fruit that will remain, so that whatever you ask the Father in my name he may give you." Significance is not about what you do for applause but what you do for the Kingdom. It's the quiet conversations, the acts of service no one sees, the love you pour into your family, the compassion you show to a stranger.

Reflection: Where in your life are you making an impact that may go unnoticed by the world but matters deeply to God?

E – Everywhere

Your worth and calling are not limited to certain roles or spaces. You carry your light everywhere. Matthew 5:14 states, "You are the light of the world. A city set on a mountain cannot be hidden." Whether you are leading a boardroom meeting, standing in line at the grocery store, tucking in a child at night, or encouraging a friend over coffee, you have the opportunity to live out your significance. Every place you are can be a place of purpose. Every moment you live can create an impact.

Reflection: Identify one space in your life where you can be more intentional about living out your calling this week.

Remember, when you choose to RISE; to **R**ealize your worth, embrace your **I**ndividual uniqueness, live with **S**ignificance, and do it **E**verywhere, you step into the abundant life God has designed for you. This is not about perfection. It's about presence. It's about showing up fully, with confidence that God placed you exactly where you are for a reason.

A Prayer for RISE

Lord, open my eyes to the truth of who I am in You. Help me to embrace my individuality as Your unique creation. Remind me that my life holds significance, not because of what I achieve, but because of who You are in me. Give me the courage to live out my calling everywhere You place me. Amen.

Your RISE Challenge

Here is your RISE challenge to help you **RISE**:

R: Journal one truth you've realized about your God-given worth.

____

____

____

____

I: List three traits or strengths that make you unique.

____

____

____

____

S: Identify one act of significance you can do this week, seen or unseen.

____

____

____

____

E: Choose one new place to intentionally live out your purpose.

____

____

____

____

Know that you were never meant to blend in or go unnoticed. You were meant to RISE; realizing your value, embracing your individuality, living your significance, and carrying it everywhere.

Reflection

- What does "rising" mean in your life right now?
- Which step of the RISE framework challenges you most?
- How can you put this framework into practice this week?

Prayer

Lord, thank You for practical tools that draw me closer to You. Help me commit to rising with courage and faith each day. Amen.

As you complete this section of the book, I challenge you to really discern what your relationship with God is. Is He someone you fear? Do you seek His wisdom? Do you consider Him a friend? How often do you have conversations with Him? Do you even hear Him speak to you? Jesus wants you to call Him friend, to lean on Him and to trust in Him. As you work through each question, ask Jesus what He thinks. Listen for His answer. Know that He loves you.

R — **REALIZE**
Awaken to your God-given value

I — **INDIVIDUAL**
Embrace what makes you unique

S — **SIGNIFICANCE**
Know that your life matters

E — **EVERYWHERE**
Live out your purpose daily

Facing Fear and Overcoming Self: Confronting doubt and fear to embrace bold living

"For God did not give us a spirit of cowardice but rather of power and love and self-control."
—2 Timothy 1:7

Most often we are the ones holding ourselves back. We feel fear; fear of failure, fear of not being good enough, fear of being overwhelmed or overworked, fear of not being liked, fear of standing out in a negative way and much, much more. Throughout my education as a coach, plus by personal experience, I have learned that the greatest roadblock to success is fear caused by yourself. This is known as self-sabotage. Boy, have I lived it. Not so much that I didn't know that I had worth, but for the fact that I allowed other people to define my worth. How could they even know my worth when they did not know me? This brings into my mind (and heart) Jeremiah 1:5, "Before I formed you in the womb I knew you, before you were born I dedicated you, a prophet to the nations I appointed you." This is why one of the fundamental concepts I teach is to know yourself.

Some of the basic things that we allow to hold us back are perfectionism, procrastination, limiting beliefs, Imposter Syndrome and fear of success. Many of these live together within us. Let's take a look at what these are:

Perfectionism: The drive to do everything flawlessly can be a form of self-sabotage. No person is flawless. Setting impossibly high standards can lead to failure, confirming our underlying fear of not being good enough. We allow social media to feed this. People show the "perfect" side of their life without showing the challenges they have faced and still face, leading us to believe we are "less than." In what areas of your life do you practice perfectionism?

____

____

____

Procrastination: This is often a coping mechanism for fear. Delaying a task, especially a new and challenging one, protects us from potential negative outcomes. It preserves the idea that success was possible if attempted. This has always been a favorite of mine. It takes hard work to push through it. Are you using procrastination as a form of a safety net? If so, in what areas of your life?

____

____

____

Limiting beliefs: These are core assumptions about yourself and the world that prevent goal achievement. For example, the belief "I'm not good enough" can prevent you from applying for a promotion or pursuing a new passion. Obviously, if you do not have the basic requirements or something equal to that, you may not be a good fit. But, giving yourself reasons why you don't measure up without considering why you do is a limiting belief. What limiting beliefs do you hold for yourself?

____

Impostor Syndrome: This psychological pattern, common among high-achievers, involves persistent self-doubt and the fear of being exposed as a "fraud." Even when presented with evidence of their success, people with Impostor Syndrome dismiss their accomplishments as luck. Now, being a Christian, I don't believe in luck. That said, the term, although it became very popular, Imposter Syndrome, is something I do not like. I did write a social media post about it. I think it places too much significance on a person who lacks self confidence as well as belief in self, founded in the fact that they just don't truly know and understand who they are. In what areas of your life do you feel "less than" or like an imposter?

____

____

____

Fear of Success: This may seem less common than fear of failure. The fear of success is also self-inflicted and blocks us from moving forward. It can be caused by a fear of increased responsibility, new expectations, or the feeling of being isolated at the top. The "what if" can truly deter us from moving forward, especially if we feel all too comfortable where we are at. What areas in your life does fear of success stop you from moving forward?

____

____

____

How do you overcome these? Well, before I introduce you to those solutions I want to talk about Positive Intelligence®. I was introduced to this scientifically based concept and chosen to participate in the coaching grant. This helped me to further understand how I was wired to think and how I can work on re-wiring my thoughts. This information is owned by Shirzad Chamine, author of the New York Times bestselling book, Positive Intelligence, and Stanford lecturer. Although I am not certified by him, I wholeheartedly believe in his techniques. I have experienced them myself and still use what I was taught through his program. I have read his book and use it as a resource. I highly recommend taking the Saboteur assessment located at https://www.positiveintelligence.com/.

The concepts taught by Positive Intelligence® are similar to what I discussed above, but are based on scientific research. We all know that our mind is a powerful thing, but that power can be used in a negative way. I like to think of it as a little devil (bad) and a little angel (good) sitting on your shoulder arguing to get you to do what they want. Ultimately, the choice is yours. It is often easier to just give in to negative beliefs. Life does take work. Staying positive takes work. Reaching for your dreams takes work. You are worth the work!

So what can you do to stay positive, push forward and reach your dreams to live with joy? Well, for starters, you need to kick that little devil off of your shoulder and silence those negative thoughts. Completing the work in the prior chapters provides a positive foundation to work on. Overcoming negative thoughts is not only a daily challenge, but most likely you will face this challenge several times a day. Constantly facing the negativity of society can make this a real challenge unless you develop your *Mental Fitness*.

What is Mental Fitness? It is a state of psychological and emotional well-being that provides you with tools and resilience to manage life's challenges, adapt to change, and maintain a healthy mind despite stress or setbacks. There will always be challenges, stress and setbacks. It is how we handle it that makes the difference on whether or not we move forward to live boldly.

How do you build your mental fitness? It is done with intentionality. Just like you are conscious of the foods you eat and make time for exercise to maintain a healthy body, you need to be intentional about what your mind consumes and also exercise it. Let's first talk about mental consumption. What kinds of things do you listen to in the car? How much TV do you watch? What kinds of shows or movies do you watch? What kinds of conversations do you have? What kinds of books or magazines do you read? In this scenario, think of your mind as a stomach. When you ingest things that are not good, they often come out in a negative way. The same thing happens with your mind. When your mind consumes a lot of negativity, negativity comes out. That can be by ingesting the negativity of violent or hate-filled shows (the news is good for that), listening to music with negative or harmful lyrics and listening to negative people around you. Negativity breeds negativity. Society has taught us to always find what is wrong and to focus on it. So how do you change that? Build your Mental Fitness.

Tips for Building Mental Fitness

1. Create a stronger thought process. Focus on controlling your thoughts. Start small. Take two minutes to just sit and breathe, focusing on breathing. Block out other noises and distractions. Taking two minutes three times a day helps you build your mental muscles so you can control your thoughts. I highly recommend Positive Intelligence® as a reference tool.
2. Feed your mind positivity. Listen to empowering podcasts and music. Read books to educate and uplift.

3. Surround yourself with positive people talking about positive things.
4. Always look for the gift or opportunity in every situation.
5. Spend time with God. Pray, read and reflect on scripture. Just be with Him.

To face your fear and to overcome self, you must be able to recognize what is getting in your way. It is much easier when you truly know yourself. Afterall, every human is flawed, but we are all fabulous.

Spend time reflecting on your fears and negative thoughts. Develop a plan to overcome them. Seek help if you need it. Set a plan to build mental fitness daily. The inner struggle can be a daily battle. Having an accountability partner will help you make progress.

Reflection

- What fears most often hold you back?
- How do you tend to rely on self instead of God?
- What might change if you trusted God fully with those fears?

Prayer

Father, I give You my fears. Replace them with Your peace and strength. Help me overcome self-reliance and walk boldly with You. Amen.

Walking with God

Start and end each day with time spent with God. It can be a prayer, silent meditation or reading scripture. Make sure you sprinkle in some gratitude, letting God know all you are grateful for. If possible, do it several times throughout the day. This can help keep you focused on what is positive. You can pray a line from scripture or even make a simple prayer like, "God, please guide me in my thoughts, words and actions. I long to be more like you. In Jesus' name I pray. Amen."

ALIGN: LIVING IN HARMONY WITH GOD'S DESIGN

Speaking Life: Affirmations & Prayer – Aligning your thoughts and words with God's truth.

The Power of the Spoken Word

Words matter. What we speak can shape our thoughts, actions, and destiny. Words can tear a person down. They stomped out my natural curiosity and caused me to keep silent. They chipped away at my self value and my self confidence. It wasn't until I started using affirmations as a teenager that I really felt the impact of positive words. I have also experienced first hand how speaking love and positivity to a person can impact their life. It can give someone the value they cannot yet find. Remember Proverbs 18:21, "Death and life are in the power of the tongue; those who choose one shall eat its fruit."

We know through Genesis 1 that God spoke creation into being. Good can overcome evil. But the good must be more prevalent. We know the world and society are constantly telling us what is wrong with us. Matthew 12:37 tells us that "By your words you will be acquitted, and by your words you will be condemned." Let's keep the positivity, beginning with affirmations!

What Are Affirmations?

Affirmations are intentional, positive statements that affirm truth about yourself, your life, or your faith. These are facts unlike wishful thinking or empty self-talk. They are not about what you want to be, but rather about what is. Then there are *secular affirmations* and *faith-based affirmations*. Secular affirmations are more socialized. For example, I am pretty or I am strong. Faith-based affirmations are rooted in scripture. As a coach, I have generally guided people with secular affirmations. I am shifting as I experience an awakening and I align my life. Utilizing scripture for affirmations is substantiated in Romans 10:17, "Thus faith comes from what is heard, and what is heard comes through the word of Christ." Faith-based affirmations are supported by Philippians 4:8, "Finally, brothers, whatever is true, whatever is honorable, whatever is just, whatever is pure, whatever is lovely, whatever is gracious, if there is any excellence and if there is anything worthy of praise, think about these things."

Why Affirmations Matter for Christians

Affirmations renew the mind and align our thinking with God's Word when based in scripture. They help us combat lies of the enemy and negative self-talk. The world is full of negativity and the enemy is quick to leverage it. Faith-based affirmations anchor us in God's promises, not shifting emotions. Romans 12:2 tells us, "Do not conform yourselves to this age but be transformed by the renewal of your mind, that you may discern what is the will of God, what is good and pleasing and perfect." The Bible is a grand resource. It is a blueprint of how we became, who we are, the value we bring and how to bring the value God gave us. Joshua 1:8 reminds us, "Do not let this book of the law depart from your lips. Recite it by day and by night, that you may carefully observe all that is written in it; then you will attain your goal; then you will succeed."

The Science Meets Scripture

We know that through neuroplasticity we can rewire our neural pathways through repetition. When I took the course offered by Positive Intelligence®, it became more clear how repetitive positive actions, thoughts and words build positive outcomes. I experienced the shift myself when I went through the program. There is a connection to biblical meditation and faith-based affirmations. Biblical meditation is not about emptying the mind, but rather filling it with God's Word and His promises. Meditation can lead to the formulation of affirmations. It involves internalizing and dwelling on specific truths from the Bible. From that, you can create biblically based affirmations, positive words of who you are in Jesus.

Thinking affirmations is not enough. It is easy for the negative thoughts to take over and push positivity right out of your mind. First write them down. You can even journal about them. You must say them out loud. Ideally, you would say them out loud to yourself in the mirror, making eye contact as you speak. Say them multiple times and say them with conviction, even if you don't truly believe them yet. When you state your affirmations, say them with the knowledge of Mark 11:23, "Amen, I say to you, whoever says to this mountain, 'Be lifted up and thrown into the sea,' and does not doubt in his heart but believes that what he says will happen, it shall be done for him." Let your affirmations be done to you.

How to Create Faith-Based Affirmations

Intentionally and prayerfully creating faith-based affirmations will give you more focused and personal results. Follow the process below. Revisit it as needed. Maintaining a written record creates an easier way to review and recreate as well as discerning its effectiveness. I recommend starting with three affirmations. If you have difficulty creating three, start with one or two. Remember John 8:32 states, "and you will know the truth, and the truth will set you free."

- **Step 1:** Identify the lie or limiting belief you want to replace. Write it (them) down!
- **Step 2:** Find a corresponding truth from Scripture. Write it down next to the corresponding lie or limiting belief.
- **Step 3:** Write your affirmation in the present tense, personal, and powerful. It is about YOU!
- **Step 4:** Keep it short and memorable. You want to be able to say your affirmations anywhere and any time you may need them.
- **Step 5:** Speak it daily with conviction. Speak them out loud in front of a mirror, making eye contact with yourself, at least once a day.

Here is an example:

Lie: "I'm not good enough."

Truth: Ephesians 2:10, "For we are his handiwork, created in Christ Jesus for the good works that God has prepared in advance, that we should live in them."

Faith-based affirmation: "I am God's masterpiece, created for a purpose."

Implementing Affirmations in Daily Life

After you have created your faith-based affirmations, you must implement them. Creating habits will help create the biggest impact. Consider these:

- Morning routine: Start the day with your list of affirmations. Remember, speak them out loud in front of the mirror while making eye contact with yourself.
- Prayer time: Integrate affirmations into prayer, speaking God's Word back to Him. Carve out a set time for prayer every day.

- Visual reminders: Post them on mirrors, desks, or phone wallpapers. You can even write them on the side or corner of your mirror so you can be reminded of them every time you pass by.
- Journaling: Write affirmations daily for reinforcement. Repetition is a great way to remember something. You can also meditate about the affirmation and write down your thoughts and feelings. This will give you a record of your thoughts and emotions have changed.

Another thought is teaching children and family to speak life by sharing affirmations about them. Get into the practice of affirming each other daily. When you use scripture to create your affirmations, you are following Deuteronomy 6:6–9 which reads, "Take to heart these words which I command you today. Keep repeating them to your children. Recite them when you are at home and when you are away, when you lie down and when you get up. Bind them on your arm as a sign and let them be as a pendant on your forehead. Write them on the doorposts of your houses and on your gates." Keep God's words before you daily. Share His words with others.

Overcoming Resistance and Doubt

Isaiah 55:11 teaches us, "So shall my word be that goes forth from my mouth; It shall not return to me empty, but shall do what pleases me, achieving the end for which I sent it." God's Word will not return void. Oftentimes when someone first begins with affirmations, they feel awkward, fake or like they are an imposter. This is why consistency and persistence matters. The enemy will fight your words and try to take away your God-given power. These feelings are a type of spiritual warfare.

The devil wants you. The less empowered you feel, the more you may reach out for an easy solution. You may give in to your feelings of inadequacies or reach for something to mask these feelings. You may succumb to depression or self medication. You may always feel that you need something more. Your focus is drawn away from God and the beautiful person He created you to be. Lean on and into God's promises, not your feelings. Here are some scripture that you can lean on:

Psalm 28:7, "The LORD is my strength and my shield, in whom my heart trusts. I am helped, so my heart rejoices; with my song I praise him."

Psalm 18:2-3, "He said I love you, LORD, my strength, LORD, my rock, my fortress, my deliverer, My God, my rock of refuge, my shield, my saving horn, my stronghold!"

2 Corinthians 12:9, "'but he said to me, 'My grace is sufficient for you, for power is made perfect in weakness.' I will rather boast most gladly of my weaknesses, in order that the power of Christ may dwell with me."

Psalm 73:26, "Though my flesh and my heart fail, God is the rock of my heart, my portion forever."

Deuteronomy 31:6, "Be strong and steadfast; have no fear or dread of them, for it is the LORD, your God, who marches with you; he will never fail you or forsake you."

Philippians 4:13, "I have the strength for everything through him who empowers me."

Isaiah 41:10, "Do not fear: I am with you; do not be anxious: I am your God. I will strengthen you, I will help you, I will uphold you with my victorious right hand."

Exodus 15:2, "My strength and my refuge is the LORD, and he has become my savior. This is my God, I praise him; the God of my father, I extol him."

1 Chronicles 16:11, " Rely on the mighty LORD; constantly seek his face."

Ephesians 6:10, " Finally, draw your strength from the Lord and from his mighty power."

Speaking Your Way into God's Plan

Understand and implement Job 22:28, "What you decide shall succeed for you, and upon your ways light shall shine." See affirmations as more than self-help. They are **faith declarations**. These were given to you by God to use. The more you speak God's truth, the more your heart and life align with His will.

I have provided for you a quick-start and a worksheet page to help you get started. Here are some tips for using this chart:

- Personalize the wording: Make the affirmation feel like your own.
- Speak aloud daily: Morning and night, or during prayer time.
- Write them down: In a journal, on sticky notes, or as phone reminders.
- Pray them back to God: Turn them into declarations of faith.
- Teach them to others: Share with family, friends, and children.

Faith-Based Affirmations Quick-Start Chart

Lie or Limiting Belief	Biblical Truth (Scripture)	Faith-Based Affirmation
I'm not good enough.	*Ephesians 2:10* – "For we are God's handiwork, created in Christ Jesus to do good works..."	I am God's masterpiece, created for a purpose.
I can't do this.	*Philippians 4:13* – "I can do all things through Christ who strengthens me."	I am empowered to do all things through Christ.
No one loves me.	*Romans 8:38–39* – "Nothing can separate us from the love of God."	I am fully loved by God, now and forever.
I'm too broken to be used by God.	*2 Corinthians 5:17* – "If anyone is in Christ, the new creation has come..."	I am made new in Christ, and He can use me for His glory.
I'm afraid of what's ahead.	*2 Timothy 1:7* – "For God has not given us a spirit of fear, but of power, love, and a sound mind."	I walk boldly in God's power, love, and peace of mind.
I'm a failure.	*Proverbs 24:16* – "Though the righteous fall seven times, they rise again..."	I rise again because God upholds me.
I have no purpose.	*Jeremiah 29:11* – "For I know the plans I have for you..."	God has a plan and purpose for my life, and I walk in it.
I'm all alone.	*Deuteronomy 31:6* – "The Lord your God goes with you; He will never leave you nor forsake you."	I am never alone—God is always with me.
My past defines me.	*Isaiah 43:18–19* – "Forget the former things; do not dwell on the past..."	My future is bright because God is doing a new thing in me.
Things will never get better.	*Romans 8:28* – "In all things God works for the good of those who love Him..."	God is working all things for my good and His glory.

Faith-Based Affirmation Worksheet

Find some quiet time and a quiet space. Be open and honest with yourself.

<u>Affirmation 1</u>

Identify and write down the lie or limiting belief you want to replace.

____

____

Find a corresponding truth from Scripture and write it here.

____

____

Write your affirmation in the present tense, personal, and powerful. It is about YOU!

____

____

<u>Affirmation 2</u>

Identify and write down the lie or limiting belief you want to replace.

____

____

Find a corresponding truth from Scripture and write it here.

____

____

Write your affirmation in the present tense, personal, and powerful. It is about YOU!

____

____

Affirmation 3

Identify and write down the lie or limiting belief you want to replace.

____

____

Find a corresponding truth from Scripture and write it here.

____

____

Write your affirmation in the present tense, personal, and powerful. It is about YOU!

____

____

Here is some extra space to write down any thoughts you may have:

____

____

____

____

____

____

____

____

____

____

Reflection

- What words do you speak most often over yourself?
- How do affirmations rooted in God's Word differ from self-talk?
- What one faith-filled affirmation can you begin speaking daily?

Prayer

Lord, let the words of my mouth reflect Your truth. Teach me to speak life over myself and others. Amen.

<u>*Walking with God*</u>

Picture this chapter as an exercise of actually walking (or sitting) with God. When you name your limiting belief, hear God's words to you. Imagine Jesus walking up to you and inviting you for a conversation. He says, "My Father loves you as I do. He created you to be good. He wants me to remind you of the gifts He gave you and the goodness in you." Then Jesus shares all God has given you. He reminds you of the gift you are to the world because God created you to be uniquely you. Hear the words. Feel the love. Embrace them.

The Whole Wellbeing (Mind, Body, Spirit): Nurturing every part of yourself as God intended.

"Do you not know that your body is a temple of the holy Spirit within you, whom you have from God, and that you are not your own? For you have been purchased at a price. Therefore, glorify God in your body." —1 Corinthians 6:19-20

I am going to start with a story. Overall, I am a healthy person. I drink on occasion and I don't smoke. I don't regularly exercise, but I do try to get my steps in every day. I am aware that I could easily become diabetic even though I don't live a terrible lifestyle. Let's face it, we are living in a society that still really doesn't promote healthy living. I have dealt with a couple of issues, one while writing this book.

I have allergies. Most are generic and non life-threatening. I was tested at the same time I had my son tested when he was a child. I live with some of my allergies-cats, dogs and dust. They are an inconvenience like making me sneeze and giving me a stuffy nose. One day I got hives all over my body. I took an antihistamine, got some rest and they went away. It happened again. The hives were my only symptom. I was working in a very stressful work environment. I was stressed out. My body let me know it. I had to learn to manage the stress through relaxation techniques such as breathing and prayerful meditation to keep them at bay. That was a learning experience. I was not in a place where I could switch jobs and I really didn't want to. I needed to learn how to deal with the stressor.

Most recently, I had a horrific scare. It started smaller. I felt something bite me (I was in a building). I began to itch and got hives. I had hives before. This time, my lips started to swell. I went to the store and bought some antihistamine and it calmed down. The second time was worse. I did start carrying antihistamine with me. It started with an itch. I don't remember a bite. I got hives all over my body and my face. I felt swelling in my inner ear. My heart was racing. I went and laid down until it passed. My sister wanted to call an ambulance, but I refused because I did not have health insurance. After it passed, I went home, took more antihistamine and slept. It went away.

The third time was different. I felt an itch that felt like a bump on my lower back. I asked my friend if there was something there. She said yes, it looks like a bite. I looked at my body and in the mirror and did not see any hives. The roof of my mouth started to swell. My inner ears then felt like they were swelling. I immediately took two antihistamines and called my husband to come get me. It only got worse. My body was being attacked. I could not control it. I vomited and fell off a chair. As I was being escorted to the bathroom, I fell again. It took two people to escort me to the bathroom. I was not at home. I declined an ambulance since I did not have insurance. Because I was wearing my watch that tracks my heart rate, I know it climbed to 138 before it dropped drastically. My body was going into shock and shutting down. Thankfully, an ambulance was called against my wishes. They gave me fluids and an epinephrine drip and then rushed to the emergency room at the closest hospital. My life was saved.

Why did I share this story? Because I was putting a dollar value on my life. God does not do that. My body, my whole self, is a gift from God and I am required to take care of it gratefully. I have shared both physical and mental (emotional) situations where more care was needed than I gave myself. Let's talk about this.

The Whole Wellbeing

When was the last time you checked on your own wellbeing? What does that even mean? Sure, we understand what it means when someone asks us how we are doing. We usually answer in a general sense, "fine". Sometimes, we even talk about it. We tell them about a particularly rough day or a recent happy experience. But that is not it! As you can see from the above shared story, there is more than just being "fine" and making it through life.

Many people wrap wellbeing into five areas: career wellbeing, social wellbeing, financial wellbeing, physical wellbeing and community wellbeing. I add sixth and seventh areas that people shy away from: mental wellbeing and spiritual wellbeing. Your health is an important gift from God so let's spend some time evaluating your whole wellbeing.

<u>Career Wellbeing</u>

I like to refer to this as Purpose Wellbeing. Makes more sense. The definition of career is "an occupation or profession" while purpose means "the reason for which something exists". Wouldn't you rather live your life for the reason you exist instead of for an occupation or profession?

When choosing a career, we often consider what skillsets we have acquired, maybe what we have learned to do well or can learn to do well, how much money we can earn doing it and if we are smart; we may even consider if we like it or if it will bring some happiness. Now a purpose is not something we CHOOSE. Purpose is something we were meant to do. Do not get me wrong, the two can align and when they do, it is the best outcome ever!

So how do you find your purpose? It is a journey. It does not have to be hard, but most likely it will take time and some true introspection. God has gifted each one of us with unique innate talents. These are different from skills that we learn. Although we can sometimes use skills to imitate innate talents, there is a difference. There are some assessments that can start you in the right direction, but your lived experiences can also help you figure it out. Go back and review the chapter "Who are You?" to help you determine if you are living your purpose. If you need help, consider investing in a Life Coach. This is a personal investment that you will reap benefits from for years.

Reflections: *Are you living your purpose or living a career? Are you fulfilled? Do you feel drained at the end of the day or do you feel energized?*

____

____

____

____

Social Wellbeing

We are social beings, even introverts need people. No matter where we find "our people"; family, friends, work, we need friendship or companionship. If we thought otherwise, the pandemic sure showed us how much we need it by forcing us to be less social. It helped us to create ways to be social without being face-to-face. Think about your social wellbeing. Remember that we are all individuals, so this looks different for everyone. Some people need a lot of friends, people they can share many different things with. Some people only need a couple of close friends. Some people might be fine just with family.

Another thing to consider is who is in your inner circle? These are the people who influence you. They provide approval, disapproval, encouragement, support and accountability. Do these people share your values? Do they have similar goals? Do they speak positively or are they constantly negative? The people you spend the most time with will shape you. They will influence your actions, your thoughts and your desires.

Reflections: *Who is part of your social circle? Are you receiving enough socialization? Do you have a confidante? Do you have someone to have fun with? Someone to help keep the sanity?*

____

____

____

____

Financial Wellbeing

We measure financial wellbeing by how our finances are managed. Does the thought of money make you feel sick or worried? Do you need to spend it as soon as you get it for fear there won't be any?

Having financial stability makes life easier. I know, duh! We are always pushed to buy on credit. The latest fads are payday loans. Get a loan now because you cannot make it to payday. This is a road to disaster because it will take you MANY paydays to pay it off! Then there is the old "keeping up with the Joneses." That is when you need to have what everyone else has even if you cannot afford it.

The best thing you can do for your wellbeing is to live WITHIN your means. That is defined as you have money to pay your bills, money to save for emergencies, money to save for the next big purchase and money to treat yourself. The answer to this is living with a budget. Yes, it is hard;

but it is the easiest way to see your income, track expenses, follow goals and meet your needs.

According to an article published in the journal "Family Relationships", the number one predictor of whether you'll end up divorced is arguing about money early in your relationship. A budget brings everything out into the open. Both people know what money is coming in and where it is going. This makes having factual discussions easier.

We were each brought up with ideas about what money means and what it can do. Some were raised with scarcity while others were raised with abundance. All of these beliefs affect how you view money and give money some control over your life. If you have feelings tied to money, you would most likely benefit from a financial coach. The right coach can help you discover your cause for the relationship you have with money and help you overcome its control over you. They can also help you create a budgeting process that works for you.

Reflections: *How does money make you feel? Do you have a fear of losing everything because you are living beyond your means? Do you have money saved? Do you utilize a budget? Is money something to attain or is it a tool to fuel your purpose?*

____

____

____

____

<u>Physical Wellbeing</u>

This one is easy. Do you have the energy, stamina, and health to live your life? What foods do you consume? Do you feed your body or are you feeding your feelings? A healthy well-balanced diet is important to ensure energy and proper brain function. Plus, we all feel better when we think we look better. What about exercise? To have healthy lungs and heart takes exercise. All of your body parts need oxygen. Keeping your brain well-oxygenated helps increase effectiveness of the brain, specifically memory. Exercise also increases energy and better sleep. All of these contribute to physical wellbeing. There are many resources to help in this area without resorting to fad diets which do more harm in the end.

There is also routine maintenance and care. We set aside time and money to care for our vehicles, but often do not invest in our own physical care. Do you have a maintenance schedule for your physical self? It's best to not wait until there is something drastically wrong. 1 Corinthians 6;19-20 reminds us, "Do you not know that your body is a temple of the holy Spirit within you, whom you have from God, and that you are not your own? For you have been purchased at a price. Therefore, glorify God in your body."

Reflections: *Are you overweight? Do you suffer from medical conditions that could be managed with a proper diet and/or exercise? Is your memory suffering? Do you feel tired or fatigued? Do you get medical care, including dental and vision?*

____

____

____

____

<u>Mental Wellbeing</u>

This topic is finally being addressed as it should be. This is a normal concern and should never be taboo or cause embarrassment. Life can be hard and we all cope in different ways. What you need to know is that this is an area you can make stronger before you even notice it is weak! People have emotions. It is ok to feel. What makes a difference is how you put those feelings into action. In this fast-paced world, stress is abundant. If you suffer from stress, anger, self-doubt or other constant emotions, learn tactics to address the symptoms and then work on the underlying issues.

It doesn't matter if you learn meditation, deep breathing techniques or how to go to a happy place if the need to do so occurs frequently. You need to find the cause. Really examine situations where these feelings arise and look for the causes. Once you find the causes, you need a plan to address them or find a solution. Building your Mental Fitness is a great way to help you manage thoughts and emotions. This may not be something you can do alone. Please always seek help if your situation is something you cannot handle or if you feel hopeless.

Reflections: *How are you feeling emotionally? Do you have extreme highs or lows? Do you feel angry, lost or forgotten? Do you believe in yourself? Can you control your thought patterns or do they control you?*

<u>Community Wellbeing</u>

Community wellbeing has to do with where you live. Do you like where you live? Does it suit your personality? Do you spend time enjoying your community by getting involved and getting to know your neighbors? Your community, where you live, plays a big part in your happiness.

If you are an outdoorsy person, you will most likely be happy living amongst some nature or at least close enough to go enjoy it. If you are a person who likes to shop often, a suburban area close to shopping plazas or malls will bring joy even as you drive by. If you like to spend more time alone than surrounded by people, you may want to live farther out in a rural area where drop-ins are less likely to happen. What is most important is that your community brings you joy when you drive through it as well as spending everyday living in it.

Reflections: *How do you feel about your community? Is it home or do you spend your time thinking of moving? Is it a place you want to be involved in or hide from?*

____

____

____

____

<u>Spiritual Wellbeing</u>

There are many religions and faiths including agnostics. Whatever your belief is, it is an important part of you. It helps to make you who you are. That said, it should be cared for like the other six parts of your wellbeing.

Examining your core beliefs, determine what is the foundation. Is this something you decided or something you have been told and just accepted? Is this something you are unsure about? If it is yours to the extent that you claim it, how can you develop it? You can practice your faith; you can enrich your understanding and knowledge of your faith. If you determine that it was "forced" upon you and is not really your belief, you can explore your options through education and talking with different people.

We are spiritual beings even if we choose to not have faith in God. Spirituality is based on spirit which definition is stated as "the principle of conscious life; the vital principle in humans." So, find out where the foundation of your conscious life is and enrich and empower it. Develop it and care for it just like the rest of yourself.

Reflections: *Is your spirituality developed? Do you spend time enriching or growing your spirituality? How does your spirituality make you, you?*

____

____

____

____

All Areas Make You Who You Are

All seven of these areas of wellbeing make you the person you are. They also can be enriched and fed to further your fulfillment. Consider working with a coach or a variety of coaches. There are great coaches that can help you in all areas of wellbeing. Aren't you worth the investment?

Reflection

- Which part of your wellbeing needs the most attention right now—mind, body, or spirit?
- How does honoring your whole self glorify God?
- What small step can you take today to nurture balance?

Prayer

Creator God, You made me whole. Help me honor You with my mind, body, and spirit in all I do. Amen.

Walking with God

Would God approve of how you have taken care of your whole self? After spending time in prayer and reflecting on your current and past wellbeing, what has God said to you? I encourage you to listen for guidance. Ask the Holy Spirit to guide your reflection and your action to care for your whole wellbeing.

Let's Talk About Growth (and Seasons of Life): Embracing God's timing through life's changing seasons.

Let's talk about Growth!

Growth was my Word of 2022. It was both something I aimed to do and something I NEEDED to do. As I was taking on more responsibilities and expanding my skills, I was constantly reminded to use GROWTH as a point of focus and as a foundation. Afterall growth without an intentional direction can just lead to ***distraction.*** There is enough distraction in this world.

I do enjoy using acronyms. It makes the work more fun and the steps easier to remember. So I started thinking about what the letters of GROWTH would mean to me. After some thought, I came up with: **G**iving, **R**esources, **O**thers, **W**isdom, **T**alent, **H**ealth.

Let's uncover each word to convey how it relates to GROWTH and how you can use it in a positive way.

Giving.

Giving is a word everyone needs to understand. Three definitions I found through a Google search are:

1. Freely transfer the possession of (something) to (someone); hand over to.

2. Cause or allow (someone or something) to have (something, especially something abstract); provide or supply with.

3. Carry out or perform (a specified action).

These definitions are common when we think about people giving. They are definitely things that everyone should practice and they do indeed lead to growth. BUT......I believe this fourth definition is what I was looking for:

4. Alter in shape under pressure rather than resist or break. When we give, our state alters....we GROW!! Think about how you are altered by giving, causing you to grow. Reflect how your giving inspires growth.

____

____

____

____

Resources.

Reviewing the definition for resource by a Google search, I found these two:

1. A stock or supply of money, materials, staff, and other assets that can be drawn on by a person or organization in order to function effectively.
2. An action or strategy which may be adopted in adverse circumstances.

So the first definition is what I think we are accustomed to using, referring to and hearing about. When I read the second definition, I thought "Wow!" Adverse circumstances definitely provide opportunity for growth, having the resource of an action or strategy is perfect!! Just like I talked about in the last chapter, challenges provide opportunity. That opportunity can definitely be growth. Working, creating and living outside of your comfort zone helps you to push your limits to become more of who you are created to be.

Think about a time when you had to deal with an adverse circumstance and how you overcame it or "grew through it." Reflect about a time you "grew through" an adverse circumstance.

____

____

____

____

<u>Others.</u>

This is something we hear a lot about. Putting others first. I will address even more in the third section of this book. I have also written several articles for my column, **_Graceful Awakening_**, hosted on <u>Patheos.com</u> that talk about this subject. Instead of focusing on "What's in it for me", focus on what you can do for others. We are enriched when we help others. We learn from others. We can gain or perfect skills by helping others. We develop emotionally when we help others. We GROW when we put the needs of others before our own. Think of a time when you were impacted by putting others first. How did that impact you? How did it help you or encourage you to grow?

____

____

____

Wisdom.

Wisdom is the soundness of an action or decision with regard to the application of experience, knowledge, and good judgment. You can understand that wisdom is something you gain over time. We need to apply our experiences, knowledge and good judgment to GROW. This is generally the reason why we look to those older than us for wisdom or to people who have "been there and done that." What if you were more intentional about applying experience, knowledge and good judgement? Your GROWTH could be quicker and more positive and even influential. PLUS you have the RESOURCE of OTHERS to lean on. Having that community to ask questions, to discuss best ways to handle things or discuss how others have maintained or acquired their results can give you a leap in WISDOM. Can you see how these activities help you GROW? Reflect on experiences of wisdom you have given and experiences you have shared.

____

____

____

Talent.

Each of us has been gifted with unique, innate talent(s). These were gifted to help each other live our purpose, just as 1Peter 4:10 tells us, "As each one has received a gift, use it to serve one another as good stewards of God's varied grace." It is true that together we are better, but we are great together when each of us is at our best! Build your innate talents with practice, knowledge and new skills. Become a better you and GROW with your innate talent! I introduced this to you earlier in this book. Know who you are and the talents you were gifted. What are your innate talents? How can you invest in them to grow?

____

____

____

____

<u>Health.</u>

We must not forget health! Obviously to grow, you need to be in good mental, spiritual and physical health. Mental health includes self-care, ample time for relaxation and rejuvenation. It also includes mental fitness to keep away the negativity. Spiritual health includes prayer, meditation, worship, praise and whatever else fits into your spiritual basis. Physical health includes diet, exercise, fluid intake and nature. You need to include all of this to ensure the best possible foundation for GROWTH. Revisit the chapter on the whole wellbeing if you need to. What ways do you invest in your overall health? What ways do you need to increase your investment in your overall health?

____

____

____

____

In discovering your GROWTH (Giving, Resources, Others, Wisdom, Talent, Health), you can determine the best ways to move forward. Do not forget to celebrate your wins, no matter how small. Know that you are worth every investment you make in yourself.

Seasons of Life

When we talk about seasons of life, we are referring to the different stages in life that can naturally occur when we are matured. Seasons of life can include singleness, marriage, motherhood, career changes, empty nest and retirement. Each one presents its own opportunities for challenges, growth and rewards. Not all seasons will apply to all people. Some people experience the seasons multiple times. Before we move forward, what season of life are you in (or seasons)?

<u>Singleness.</u>

Ahhh, singleness. This can be a great time to find yourself. Whether it is in your early adult years or even as a season even later in life. Sure there can be the challenges of loneliness or even feeling lost, but the opportunities and rewards can be great. This can be a time to really get to know yourself. You have time to invest in your skills and enjoy your hobbies. It can be a time of exploration to learn more about yourself and what talents you have to invest in. Rewards can include finding joy, enjoying quiet time and experiencing personal growth. This can be especially true if there is no one else depending on you. If you are in the Season of Singleness, ask yourself the following questions:

Reflections: Do I need to get to know myself more? If the answer is yes, reflect on how you can do that. Are you happy in this Season of Singleness? Why or why not?

____

____

____

____

Marriage.

Marriage, a union between two people. A partnership. This can sometimes be a big transition. When you totally combine two lives, compromises may need to be made. Some people are just better at compromise than others. So there are plenty of challenges, especially if things like children and finances are not discussed beforehand. Communication is key as well as being committed to each other. There are plenty of opportunities for growth. You can learn so much from your partner and yourself. The rewards are great. Having a partner in life to support you, encourage you, participate with understanding in your lows, and celebrate your highs and wins with you is priceless.

Reflections: Where are you in the Season of Marriage? What challenges do you need to overcome? What joys have you experienced? What opportunities for growth are present and how will you embrace them?

____

____

____

____

Motherhood.

Children change your life forever. There is both good and not so good. Children often take over your life as the center of everything. Women will often lose their own identities to the identity of "mom." Mom is not a bad thing. Your kids do need you, but you are still a person with her own identity. Being a mom does not define you. It is part of who you are. For most mothers, when kids are young, your life is very intertwined with your child(ren) as they are dependent on you. As they grow and learn to be their own person, moms sometimes get lost because they forgot they were a person and not only a mom. I love being a mom even as my kids are now grown with families of their own. But let's face it, moms live so the kids can be. Some challenges for moms can be less sleep, less time for themselves and giving up parts of who they are. We are actually taught that those traits make a good mother. Letting your child(ren) see the real you, is a great opportunity to teach them how to be their best selves. There are plenty of opportunities for growth during motherhood. You learn how to care and nurture another human being. You learn how to budget and how to balance schedules. I could go on. The rewards are even greater than the challenges and opportunities. Afterall, you may have created a life. You help that little human embrace their own innate talents to contribute to make the world a better place. It's really amazing.

Reflections: Where are you in the Season of Motherhood? What challenges have you faced? What challenges do you expect to face? Where have you grown as a mother and as a person because of motherhood? What other opportunities lay before you? Where have you experienced joy?

____

____

____

____

Career Changes.

Sometimes career changes happen because we want them to and other times we have no choice. Either way, it can be both stressful and exciting. Some challenges that you may have to face can include changes in pay, changes in schedules, and an additional learning curve. Opportunities can be many if you keep an open mind. These can include opportunities to learn new things or the ability to apply skills you haven't used before. Maybe the change has helped you to align your life with your purpose. There may be pay increases or a flexible schedule. The rewards will arrive based on how you embrace the opportunities.

Reflections: Why are you in a career change and how do you feel about it? How can you practice positivity if this is something you didn't want? How will you continue to develop yourself and embrace your innate talents to align your career with your purpose? What rewards have you experienced and what rewards can you look forward to?

____

____

____

____

Empty Nest.

The Season of Empty Nest can be embraced or feared. If your identity is too tightly attached to your child(ren), this can be very difficult. If you are married and are facing this season, it can present additional challenges and opportunities. An empty nest usually provides more space in the home. You can re-purpose areas or even down-size to a smaller home which may even free up more time and money. Also, you can gain more free time because you have less people immediately dependent on you and your time. Challenges can be that people just feel lost after facing the Season of Empty Nest. They may have grown apart from their spouse and fear getting reacquainted. The opportunities are many including beginning to reacquaint yourself with your spouse. You will have more time to learn new things or to engage in hobbies that you miss.

Reflections: What do you fear about the Season of the Empty Nest? What do you look forward to or what do you enjoy? How can you use this season to invest in your growth?

____

____

____

____

<u>Retirement.</u>

Many people fear the Season of Retirement and many people eagerly await it. Much like the Season of Empty Nest, it depends on where your personal identity lies. Some of the same challenges exist here. You can always continue working without having a paid job. There are many opportunities for volunteering, consulting and partaking in hobbies. The most important thing I understand about retirement is that you should not stop living. Your life as well as your time may just exist differently than before retirement.

Reflections: What do you fear about the Season of retirement? What opportunities do you see? If you are in retirement, how are you spending your time living? Are you able to live more intentionally? How?

____

____

____

____

Reflection

- What season of life are you in right now?
- How can you embrace growth even in hard seasons?
- What has God been teaching you recently?

Prayer

Father, help me embrace every season You lead me into. Grow me through challenges and remind me that You make all things beautiful in Your time. Amen.

Walking with God

No matter what season or seasons of life you are in, it is important to remain as flexible as possible to be able to embrace opportunities as they arise. Keep your faith as your foundation. Have conversations with God and let Him guide you. Always remember to trust in God's timing. It may seem like things are not happening as they should, but God has a plan!

Finding Purpose as the Key to Joy: Unlocking the deep joy that comes from living your calling.

Finding Purpose as the Key to Joy

Take a moment to sit down and just relax. Deeply breathe in. Deeply breathe out. Continue to do so as you relax into regular, rhythmic breathing. When you are relaxed, feel your heartbeat in your chest, wrist or neck. Feel that rhythm of life that God gave you. Now ask yourself, "Why did God give me this heartbeat?"

There is a truth that society often works very hard at keeping from us. This truth is that joy is not found in chasing the world's definition of success or material things, but in living out God's purpose for us. Just reflect on Ephesians 2:10, "For we are his handiwork, created in Christ Jesus for the good works that God has prepared in advance, that we should live in them." This Scripture verse clearly tells us that we are created for something special and that is how we should live. Many people stay occupied with the busyness of life and believe they are living how they were intended. They may be doing good works along the way and even developing their relationship with God, but they are not truly living for God. They are not living for the purpose God created them for. They most likely don't even know what that purpose is, so they carry on with life meeting a level of success defined by society. Internally, they have no joy. They feel unfulfilled, like life is just happening to them and they are not creating a difference. They feel insignificant.

I have lived this. We are taught to strive for financial and material success. Your family needs to earn a certain income to be able to live a certain way and buy that house, the fancy car and the newest electronic gadget. Your kids need designer clothes and should be kept busy (distracted) with lots of activities. It is just too easy to get wrapped up in that race and get distracted by material things. We are also taught to be busy. You must be a doer. Your accomplishments (or lack thereof) define you. It is true that we have a purpose to live. We were given innate talents and skills to serve with, but being busy just to be busy is another distraction. I have had to find my purpose and aim my talents and actions to fulfill it. I am still learning and refining, but I believe I am almost there.

Take a good look at your life. Do you believe you are living your purpose? What does it look like? What does it *feel* like? Spend some time reviewing your life. Think about where you have been, what you have been taught and how you have been encouraged. Take time to really evaluate where you are now in life. Evaluate your priorities and why they exist. What is your main priority? Contemplate your goals for your future and what actions you plan to take to achieve them. It may help you to write these thoughts and discoveries down. You may even want to journal about them for a few days or even more. Then you will need to evaluate how your past affects you today as well as your future. You may discover that you need to make some changes to your priorities.

Reflection

- Do you feel that inner joy even when you encounter a challenge?
- Do you know what you are doing is making a positive impact on humanity?

- Are you feeling fulfilled or does it seem something is lacking?

Prayer

Father, guide me to know your purpose for me. Please put people in my life that lead me to you. Help me to discover the person you created me to be, gifted with unique talents to serve and build up Your Kingdom. I know I was meant for more. Amen.

Walking with God

Continue building your relationship with God. He loves you and He has a plan for you. Have conversations with Him and be sure to listen for His responses. Ask the Holy Spirit to walk with you on this journey and to give you the wisdom to see the path God has laid out for you.

The F.O.C.U.S. Framework

As we all know, life provides many distractions. I have been distracted often while writing this book. It takes focus to stay on the correct path every day. This is one of the reasons I created the F.O.C.U.S. Framework. Using F.O.C.U.S as the acronym will help you remember key components to uncovering your purpose. Let's discover what **F.O.C.U.S.** means:

F – *Find*: Seek God first in prayer and discernment. Purpose is not self-invented but discovered through Him. Matthew 6:33, "But seek first the kingdom [of God] and his righteousness, and all these things will be given you besides."

O – *Original*: God designed each of us uniquely. Your purpose is not a copy of anyone else's. The world needs the YOU that YOU were created to be. Psalm 139:13–14, "You formed my inmost being; you knit me in my mother's womb. I praise you, because I am wonderfully made; wonderful are your works! My very self you know."

C – *Creative*: God is a Creator, and we reflect Him when we create. Sometimes purpose shows up in the creative ways we solve problems, serve others, or build community. Genesis 1:27, "God created mankind in his image; in the image of God he created them; male and female he created them."

U – *Unique*: You bring something no one else can. Your strengths, talents, and life experiences are intentionally yours. 1 Corinthians 12:4–6, "There are different kinds of spiritual gifts but the same Spirit; there are different forms of service but the same Lord; there are different workings but the same God who produces all of them in everyone."

S – *Solutions*: Purpose isn't just for us. It's lived out when we bring hope, healing, or answers to others' needs. Purpose is always tied to service. Matthew 5:16, "Just so, your light must shine before others, that they may see your good deeds and glorify your heavenly Father."

Joy as the Byproduct

When we live with F.O.C.U.S., we align with God's calling. Joy comes naturally. It does not come from circumstances, but from fulfilling what God made us for. For example, when someone uses their God-given gifts, even in small ways, they often feel "this is what I was made to do." That sense is joy. Even working long hours or intensely in your purpose, you tend to feel more energized instead of worn out. You want to keep doing, to keep serving using your God-given gifts.

Practical Application

You may be thinking "This is great but how do you begin?" Here are some simple steps to help you begin:

1. Journal about times you've felt most alive and purposeful.
2. Ask: What do people often come to you for help with?
3. Pray for clarity and be open to God's nudges.

I want to share a short story with you. My mother-in-law liked to do jigsaw puzzles. When we would visit her, I would sometimes try to help. She always left her puzzles in progress on the dining room table. She worked on a lot of difficult puzzles. I would try to fit pieces together that looked like they belonged, but oftentimes, they didn't just quite fit. I could tell by the difficulty I had getting the piece to lay right or by the way the colors just didn't look right, that it was the wrong piece. It just was made to fit there. Sometimes I would get frustrated, but kept trying and other times I just quit working on the puzzle. The times when I found a piece that fit, brought a smile and a great feeling of accomplishment.

I've often thought about how life is like that. For years, I tried to force myself into roles or expectations that weren't mine. It was what others told me I should do or be. I could almost make it work, but something always felt off. I often would get bored and lose interest. I would feel really unfulfilled like life was happening to me. I was not living life. It wasn't until I pursued God's design for my life that I realized I was trying to fit into someone else's space.

When I began to **Find Original Creative Unique Solutions** instead of the world's answers, I discovered where I fit because it was God's purpose for me. Life then came together with clarity and joy, just like when the puzzle pieces finally fit together to make a beautiful picture.

How This Connects to F.O.C.U.S.

Connecting F.O.C.U.S. to purpose is simple when we connect the story above.

Find: Purpose begins when we seek God's plan for us. We need to be open to possible change.

Original: Each puzzle piece has its original place, just as we have our own. We just have to find it and not force the wrong things.

Creative: Sometimes we need to think differently to see where we belong. Prayer will support this.

Unique: No two pieces are the same; just as you are not the same as another person. Your gifts are unlike anyone else's.

Solutions: Once we're in place, the whole picture (our family, community, and world) becomes clearer and stronger.

Joy isn't about fitting everywhere; it's about fitting where God designed you to be. When you discover your unique purpose, you become fulfilled by the things you do and the service you provide. Life becomes easier when you trust in God's plan for you.

Reflection

- Which part of F.O.C.U.S. resonates most with your current season?
- When have you felt most aligned with your God-given purpose?
- How does serving others bring you joy?

Prayer

Lord, thank You for creating me with purpose. Help me to focus on You, discover the unique ways You've designed me, and use them to bring joy to others. Let my life be a reflection of Your love and light. Amen.

Walking with God

Be open to what God has in store for you. You need to have trust. To have trust you need a relationship. Continue to build that relationship with God. He is waiting for you.

Reflection & Journaling Prompts for F.O.C.U.S.

<u>F – Find</u>

Reflection Questions:

- Where am I currently seeking purpose; through God, or through the world's standards?_______________________

  ____

  ____

  ____

- What practices (prayer, scripture, quiet time) help me hear God's voice most clearly? _______________________

  ____

  ____

  ____

  ____

Journaling Prompt:

Write a prayer asking God to reveal the areas of your life where you need to find His direction instead of leaning on your own understanding.

____

____

____

____

<u>O – Original</u>

Reflection Questions:

- In what ways do I sometimes compare myself to others?

  ____

  ____

  ____

  ____

- What makes me "me"; the traits or talents people often notice about me?

  ____

  ____

  ____

  ____

Journaling Prompt:

List 5 qualities, strengths, or passions that reflect how God made you original. Circle the one that surprises you the most, and thank God for it.

____

____

____

____

C – Creative

Reflection Questions:

- How have I expressed creativity in solving problems, serving others, or finding new paths?

____

____

____

____

- What might God be inviting me to create (a project, an idea, a habit, a solution)?

____

____

____

____

Journaling Prompt:

Think about a recent challenge. Brainstorm 3 creative ways you could approach it with God's wisdom instead of your usual habits.

____

____

____

____

<u>**U – Unique**</u>

Reflection Questions:

- What past experiences, even hard ones, have shaped my perspective and purpose?

  ____

  ____

  ____

  ____

- How do my CliftonStrengths® / God-given talents show up in my daily life?

  ____

  ____

  ____

  ____

Journaling Prompt:

Write about one time you felt completely "in your element." What were you doing? How did it feel? How does that moment reveal your unique calling?

____

____

____

____

S – Solutions

Reflection Questions:

- Who around me could benefit from the gifts and insights God has given me?

  ____

  ____

  ____

  ____

- How does serving others bring me joy and meaning?

  ____

  ____

  ____

  ____

Journaling Prompt:

Write about one problem in your community, church, or family. Then write down one small step you could take this week to be part of the solution.

____

____

____

____

Wrap-Up Prompt

Take a few minutes to prayerfully journal:

"Lord, thank You for giving me purpose. Show me how to focus on You daily, embrace my originality, use my creativity, live into my uniqueness, and offer solutions that bring hope and joy to others."

What is Success?
Redefining success through faith, gratitude, and God's perspective.

*"In all circumstances give thanks, for this is the will
of God for you in Christ Jesus."*
—1 Thessalonians 5:18

Success is simply defined as an accomplishment of an aim, strategy or purpose. Society has taught us that success means a large house, expensive cars, fancy clothes, a pretty person to hang from our arm, a fancy career, and lots of money. We think that once we find success, we will finally be happy. The truth is, most people keep chasing more and better. They want more homes, a better significant other, better or more cars, more money, a more significant titled career, and fancier clothes. There will always be more and better things to be had, if that is your perception of success. This is why so many "successful" people lead unhappy lives.

There are four keys to success that you can find by just doing an internet search. They generally involve setting clear goals or having a strong purpose, taking consistent action, being resilient with persistence, learning from failure, and cultivating positive relationships and a positive mindset. Other commonalities you will find are commitment, continuous growth, self-awareness, and the ability to adapt to change as well as to overcome challenges. Let's take a look at four common steps to success.

1. Set Clear Goals and Purpose

Define what success means to you by setting clear, specific goals and identifying a strong sense of purpose to guide your efforts. There are two types of goals: SMART Goals and DUMB goals. Society is quick to teach about SMART goals. It makes sense, but these goals do not necessarily lead to joy. SMART goals meet the following criteria: Specific, Measurable, Achievable/Action-Oriented, Relevant, and Time-bound. It is easy to know when you have accomplished these goals. DUMB goals are defined as Dream-driven, Uplifting, Method-friendly, and Behavior-triggered. These are the "bigger picture" goals that lead to joy. You will need both, but start with the DUMB goals and don't be afraid to dream big!

What are some **SMART** goals you can implement?

____

____

____

____

What are some **DUMB** goals you can implement?

____

____

____

____

2. Take Consistent Action

Although dreaming is extremely important, success requires more. It involves taking deliberate, daily steps and working on your plan to achieve your goals. Spend time in planning phases. Dream big. What does it look like when you have reached your goals? How do you feel?

What do you see? Write it down! This is your starting point. Work backwards, imagining how you got to each step. What did you have to do or learn to get there? Answer these questions below.

---

3. Embrace Persistence and Resilience

Know that there will be challenges. I had a friend and mentor that told me when you are doing something good, the devil will try to stop you. Having challenges may very well mean you are on the right path. You must be persistent, learn from failures, and develop the mental toughness to overcome obstacles and keep moving forward. Don't forget to pray and discern!

What do you perceive as possible challenges to the goals you set above? How can you overcome those challenges and stay resilient to your plan?

---

4. Cultivate Strong Relationships and Mindset

I have already touched on these topics earlier. You need to build positive and supportive relationships. As humans we are social beings who benefit from cooperation and teamwork. In fact, we are created to work together as we are one body, but many parts as stated in 1 Corinthians 12:12 (As a body is one though it has many parts, and all the parts of the body, though many, are one body, so also Christ.) You also need to cultivate a growth-oriented and resilient mindset. You need to believe in your ability to achieve what you desire. The chapters "Facing Fear and Overcoming Self" and "Let's Talk about Growth" will help you.

Weaving in gratitude every day of your life will make success so much sweeter and build that positive mindset.

What strong relationships will help you to achieve your goals? Is your mindset strong enough to work through and overcome challenges? What avenues will you use to seek help if you begin to struggle?

____

____

____

____

Gratitude

When thinking about gratitude, reflect on Nehemiah 8:10, "He continued: 'Go, eat rich foods and drink sweet drinks, and allot portions to those who had nothing prepared; for today is holy to our LORD. Do not be saddened this day, for rejoicing in the LORD is your strength!'"

Gratitude is when you genuinely feel thankful for good things in your life. No matter what challenges you may be facing, there is good in your life. Learn to find the good and be grateful for it. Start at the beginning of the day. If you woke up, you were just gifted another day! That is a reason to be grateful! What good things happen throughout the day? Pay attention and notice even the small things, a smile from a stranger or someone lets you out into traffic. The more you are intentional about noticing, the more goodness you will see.

Now that you are noticing the goodness, be grateful for it! Say it out loud! Say "thank you" often. Thank God for the new day. Thank the stranger for the smile. Thank a co-worker for helping you out. Thank God for your innate gifts that helped you to reach a goal. You can even start a gratitude journal where you write in it every day, documenting the good things in your life.

Start cultivating gratitude as a daily spiritual practice. Speak directly to God, thanking Him for the blessings in your life. Set reminders until it becomes a habit. Every prayer should begin with gratitude. Every day should begin and end with gratitude. Tell someone you are grateful for them and tell them why!

Share below what you are grateful for.

____

____

____

____

So what does success mean to you?

To truly create your intentional definition of success, you must know who you are and why you are. Completing the first section of this book (**Rise**) and this section (**Align**) will help you to create your definition so you can live it through the third section (**Shine**).

I pray that by the end of this book, you will have a greater understanding of your definition of success and how to live it. Share your current definition of success below.

____

____

____

____

Reflection

- How do you currently define success?
- How does God's definition of success differ from the world's?
- What are you most grateful for right now?

Prayer

Gracious God, help me see success through Your eyes. Teach me gratitude in all things and contentment in Your plan. Amen.

Walking with God

When you build a relationship with God focusing on gratitude, you will see the world differently. You will see yourself differently. You are a gift from God to the world. Continue to invite God, Jesus and the Holy Spirit to join you on your walk of life. Ask them to guide you and give you strength to shine! It is what you are meant for!

SHINE:
IMPACT, LEGACY & LIVING BOLDLY

Community, Relationships & Service: Bringing light to others through love and service.

"Just so, your light must shine before others, that they may see your good deeds and glorify your heavenly Father." —Matthew 5:16

We live in a world that craves love, connection, and meaning. Many people lack the basic love, support, and encouragement needed to shine their light. Jesus reminds us that our light is not meant to be hidden but to be shared. Our God-given gifts and talents are tools to help others. It is not about drawing attention to ourselves. It is about pointing others to God through our actions. We are to be an evangelist because we are who we are. It is about doing and giving without expectation of receiving.

The Call to Love

St. Thomas Aquinas said, "To love is to will the good of the other." Love is not a fleeting feeling; it is an intentional choice. It is deciding to act in ways that uplift, encourage, and bless another person. This is the essence of Christian service; putting God's love into motion. It is also the foundation of every good relationship. When the foundation of our relationships is love, we are always giving what will be good for others. You don't have to try to do what is right, it just comes naturally.

Sometimes it can be hard for us humans to just give love when another person is difficult. What we don't realize is that people often act or appear difficult because they are struggling. They are in need. These struggles or needs are not always easily visible to us. I challenge you to stop. Consider what struggles they may be going through or needs they may have that you are not aware of. Consider that they may be lacking love themselves or may not know how to freely give it. Be the example of Christian love. Do it with joy and do it for Jesus.

How can you share more love everyday?

____

____

____

____

Seeking God's Vision for Others

One of the most powerful ways to serve is by asking God, "How do You see this person? What is Your vision for them?" This reminds me of the song by Brandon Heath. "Give Me Your Eyes." The chorus lyrics (courtesy of Genius.com) are:

Give me Your eyes for just one second
Give me Your eyes so I can see
Everything that I keep missin'
Give me Your love for humanity
Give me Your arms for the broken-hearted
The ones that are far beyond my reach
Give me Your heart for the ones forgotten
Give me Your eyes so I can see

When we ask God to see people as He sees them, instead of seeing people only by their struggles or shortcomings, we see them as beloved children of God with immense potential.

When we pray this way, our perspective shifts. When we allow ourselves to open our eyes with our heart and mind, we can see the beauty that each person is because they were created by God to be a uniquely beautiful human. We begin to see who God created them to be.

Begin to see each person you interact with or cross paths with every day the way you believe Jesus would, with an open heart. What goodness do you see in them? In what ways do they need help or encouragement? How can you make a difference in their life? How **will** you make a difference in their life? Choose one person that you interact with in the next 24 hours and answer those questions below.

____

____

____

____

____

____

____

Living Beyond Yourself

Our culture often tells us to focus inward. It is our comfort, our success, and our happiness that is often our priority. Jesus calls us to live outward, to pour ourselves into others so that the Kingdom of God expands. True joy comes not from hoarding blessings but from sharing them. This includes our gifts and talents that help us to live our purpose. When women align with their God-given purpose, they naturally radiate light. But the question remains: How do we carry this light into the world in tangible ways?

Sometimes it is easier to start with the people closest to us like our immediate family. We feel comfortable giving and sharing to people we know. We should be able to give freely to those closest to us. But think about giving and sharing more. How can you apply the way you give to family to giving and sharing with people you are acquaintances with? How can you go one step further and give and share with people you don't know?

When we live beyond ourselves, we leave behind something greater than accomplishments; we leave behind a legacy of love that continues to ripple through generations. We leave behind memories of discipleship and how to live as a Christian. Jot down some ideas of how you can make a difference by giving or sharing with people you don't know.

____

____

____

____

Bringing Light to Others

As we journey through life, once we love ourselves and develop our God-given talents, we need to shine brightly for all to see. Actually, we should be shining while we are learning and growing. Remember, the world needs the **you** that you were created to be. So bring your light and shine it brightly. Shine it in your close, personal relationships, in your acquaintances, your community and everywhere!

What gifts or talents has God blessed you with? Consider how you can use those to enrich your relationships. Think about all of your relationships; personal, business, acquaintances and even people you don't yet know. Next consider your community. Your community can start small and then branch out. Think of your community as your family, your place of employment, the neighborhood you live in, the town or city you live in, your state, your country and then the world. Your light has the ability to grow to shine across it all. It may take time. It will definitely take work and you may never know just how far your light has reached.

A very intentional way of shining your light is through service. This brings to mind James 2:17, *"So also faith of itself, if it does not have works, is dead."* This supports the opening quote for this chapter, Matthew 5:16. Service can be small and it can also be very large. One is not necessarily better than the other. What truly matters is impact, how the service can make life better for someone else based on **their** needs. I challenge you to look around and see needs that are not being met. There will always be people who are in need of basic necessities like food, clothing and shelter. If those needs are being met by other people through outreach programs, food pantries and shelter assistance, what else do they need? Many people lose their dignity (or feel they do) in these processes. Let's face it, we humans can be very judgemental. How can you help to give them dignity? How can you help to share that they are loved, wanted and needed in society?

I do encourage you to reach out to or join organizations to help serve others. There are a lot of non-profits that exist to help people. There are even companies that provide service opportunities for their employees. Let's not forget our churches that also help in a variety of ways. In addition to serving through these organizations, I encourage you to pray about and consider how you can shine your light through service every day.

Brainstorm some ideas below:

____

____

____

____

Reflection

- Who has God placed in your life to love and serve?
- How does your faith show up in your relationships?
- Where can you shine His light in your community today?

Prayer

Lord, make me a vessel of Your love. Use me to serve others, build community, and reflect Your light in the world. Amen.

Walking with God

When we see and experience people through God's eyes and heart, we see the value in others. Ask God to give you His eyes, His heart and His ears to see each human for the valuable creation He gave to us. You can start small, but don't think small. Be open to what God has planned for you.

Leaving a Legacy: Building a life that inspires and blesses generations to come.

"The just walk in integrity; happy are their children after them!" —Proverbs 20:7

When I think about legacy, I think about the ripple effects of a life lived with intention. It's a life that points back to God. I wrote an article for my **Graceful Awakening** column, hosted on patheos.com titled "Are You a Laborer for Christ?" inspired by a homily given by Fr. Mike Schmitz. His message challenged me to ask myself a hard question: Am I working for Jesus or am I working for myself?

It's easy to get caught up in the busyness of life; pursuing goals, climbing ladders, and chasing dreams. But if we're not careful, we may end up achieving success in the world's eyes while losing sight of our eternal purpose. The TobyMac song "Lose My Soul" captures that tension perfectly: "I don't want to gain the whole world and lose my soul." That line always hits home. What are we chasing and what are we giving up in the process? What if, instead of chasing things, we focused on what we're giving. Focus on giving our time, our wisdom, our faith and our love?

A legacy rooted in Jesus is not about possessions or accomplishments. It's about impact. It's about leaving behind the light of Jesus in the hearts of others.

Living a Jesus-Centered Legacy

Leaving a legacy isn't about fame or fortune. It's about faithfulness. It's not measured in what we accumulate but in what we pour out. Every act of kindness, every prayer whispered for another, every word of encouragement are seeds of legacy.

Small, consistent choices often shine the brightest. A kind word to a struggling friend, mentoring a younger woman, or volunteering in your church or community may seem simple, but those moments are *eternal investments*. When we love as Jesus loved, we leave fingerprints of heaven on the world.

Mentoring: Sharing an Example of Faith

Mentoring is one of the most powerful ways to leave a legacy. Sharing your wisdom, your struggles, and your victories can help others recognize God's hand in their own story. True mentoring isn't about telling others what to do. True mentoring is about walking beside someone, praying with them, and helping them see who God created them to be. It's not a transaction. It is a true relationship. It creates a transformation.

Paul modeled this beautifully with Timothy. He didn't just teach him the faith, he lived it with him. Their relationship was built on love, encouragement, and truth. Through mentorship, we continue the work of discipleship that Jesus began.

Volunteering: Being the Hands and Feet of Jesus

We all have something to give. Whether it's serving at a local shelter, teaching a Bible study, or simply showing up for someone in need, volunteering allows us to be the visible expression of God's love. When we volunteer, we're not just helping others; we're cultivating humility, compassion, and gratitude within ourselves. These acts remind us that we are all part of the body of Christ, each with a role to play in His kingdom.

As Mother Teresa said, *"It's not how much we give but how much love we put into giving."* Every time you serve with love, you leave a trace of Jesus in someone's heart.

Ministry: Using Your Gifts for God's Glory

Each of us has a ministry. It may be on a stage, at a desk, in a classroom, or at the kitchen table. Ministry simply means *serving others in God's name.* When we step into the ministry God has placed before us, we honor Him and inspire others to do the same. You don't have to be a preacher or missionary to live a life of mission. Living with integrity, kindness, and faith in your workplace, home, or neighborhood can change more lives than you may ever realize.

Ask God daily:

"Lord, how can I serve You today through the gifts You have given me?"

He will show you ways to minister through your words, your work, and your witness.

Faith in Action: How Legacy Lives On

Legacy isn't built in a day. It is built over time. It is built one day at a time. The way you treat others, how you respond to challenges, and how you live out your faith when no one is watching all contribute to the story your life will tell.

Your legacy is written in the lives you touch. It's found in the children who see you pray, the friends who see your faith in trials, and the strangers who feel God's love through your smile. Jesus said in Matthew 5:16, *"Just so, your light must shine before others, that they may see your good deeds and glorify your heavenly Father."* That is the essence of a Jesus-centered legacy. We do not shine for our glory, but for His.

Reflection

- What values and truths do you want to pass on?
- How do your daily choices reflect the legacy you hope to leave?
- Who in your life are you influencing right now?

Prayer

Heavenly Father, thank You for the gift of life and the opportunity to serve You through it. Help me live each day with purpose and integrity, leaving a legacy that honors You. Let my words uplift, my actions inspire, and my faith endure through generations. May those who come after me know You more deeply because of the life I lived. In Jesus' name, Amen.

Walking with God

What are you currently chasing and is it drawing you closer to or further from God? Think about how you can be more intentional in mentoring or serving others. What legacy of faith do you want your children, friends, or community to remember? Prayerfully ask God to show you His plan. Decide on one step you can take this week to leave a lasting imprint of God's love and implement it.

Legacy Action Plan: Living a Life That Lasts

Leaving a legacy begins today. It is determined in the choices you make, the love you give, and the faith you live. You don't have to wait for a "someday" moment to start building it. God invites you to plant seeds of legacy right where you are, right now.

Here's a simple 3-step plan to help you live out your Jesus-centered legacy intentionally:

1. Live with Purpose: Rise Each Day with Intention

"Teach us to count our days aright, that we may gain wisdom of heart." —Psalm 90:12

Every morning, rise with a purpose greater than yourself. Ask, *"Lord, how can I honor You today?"* Your legacy is written in the small, faithful steps you take daily. It is in how you love, how you serve, and how you respond when no one's watching. Living with purpose means aligning your actions with God's Word and allowing your life to reflect His light in every circumstance.

Action Step:

Start each day with a prayer of alignment:

"God, use me today as Your vessel. Let my words, work, and walk glorify You."

2. Lead with Love: Align Your Life with God's Heart

"Your every act should be done with love."
—1 Corinthians 16:14

The greatest legacies are built on love; love that listens, forgives, encourages, and uplifts. When you align your life with God's heart, your actions naturally overflow with compassion and grace. Whether mentoring, volunteering, or simply being present for a friend, let your love be the evidence of Jesus within you. Remember, people may forget what you said or did, but they'll never forget how you made them feel, especially if you made them feel loved by God.

Action Step:

Each week, choose one intentional act of love. It can be to write an encouraging note, make a call, serve someone quietly, or pray for a person who needs it.

3. Leave with Impact: Shine His Light for Generations

"But those with insight shall shine brightly like the splendor of the firmament, And those who lead the many to justice shall be like the stars forever."
—Daniel 12:3

Your faith doesn't end with you. It echoes through the generations that follow. Living a legacy means investing in others, modeling faithfulness, and trusting that the seeds you plant will grow in God's timing. To leave a Jesus-centered impact, focus not on perfection but on presence. Focus on being there for others in love, faith, and truth. Your consistency in walking with God is the greatest sermon your life will ever preach.

Action Step:

Write a "Legacy Letter."
Reflect on the faith, values, and lessons you want to pass on to your children, mentees, or community. Share your story as a testimony of God's grace.

Final Reflection: Rise. Align. Shine.

Legacy is not what you leave *behind*. It's what you leave *within*. When you rise with purpose, align with love, and shine with faith, you don't just live for yourself; you live to glorify God. Every smile, every prayer, every word of encouragement becomes a thread in the tapestry of God's eternal story. You are not just living a life, you are building a legacy of light.

What legacy do you want to leave?

____

____

____

____

Start brainstorming ways to live it.

____

____

____

____

Empowerment to Live It Out:
A call to step out, live boldly, and shine with purpose.

"Go, therefore, and make disciples of all nations, baptizing them in the name of the Father, and of the Son, and of the holy Spirit, teaching them to observe all that I have commanded you. And behold, I am with you always, until the end of the age." —Matthew 28:19-20

Jesus' Great Commission is not just a suggestion, it is a command rooted in love and confidence. He didn't say, "Try if you feel ready." He said, "Go." When we surrender and live boldly in faith, we become vessels through which His light shines in the world. It is our calling to be the light.

Surrender

Surrender is not a weakness. It is the ultimate act of strength, because it requires trust. God is in control, but He does not force His control on us. We have a choice. Not everyone believes this. He is only in control if we allow Him to be. He gave us Free Will. Free Will allows us to turn away from Him whenever we choose. Why would we choose that? Go back and read the scripture above. That is how we are called to live. We are called to surrender to God's plan for us. After all, Jeremiah 29:11 reads, "For I know well the plans I have in mind for you—oracle of the LORD—plans for your welfare and not for woe, so as to give you a future of hope." Even before we were born, He had a purpose in mind for us. Jeremiah 1:5 reminds us of that: "Before I formed you in the womb I knew you, before you were born I dedicated you, a prophet to the nations I appointed you." When we surrender to God, we accept and step into that purpose instead of fighting against what God has planned for us.

Although I am still working on my surrender, I can share the fruitfulness it has brought me so far. In the past, I have been very hesitant in labeling myself as Christian or faith-based. Society is telling us that is not acceptable. Doing so may even limit your reach. I fought it. Every time I hesitated, I would reach just one person that would share with me how what I shared through faith has impacted them. It brought me joy. Little by little I started to embrace what I have felt called to do: preach through writing, talking and social media. I use preach in a way to mean educate, share, and uplift others. More doors have opened for me. This book is the best example with more to come. I have two other books in progress; one is a book for mothers and their daughters and another will include a spiritual growth assessment. This has been a journey that I needed to surrender for.

Surrendering is hard. As humans we are taught to be in control, to be the one in power. Know that you always have control and power. You can always say no. Where will a no take you? Where will a yes take you? More specifically, where will a yes to God take you? Spend some time reflecting on your past decisions.

Was there a time you said no and you wondered what would happen if you said yes? Jot some thoughts about what could have happened.

____

____

____

____

____

____

____

____

Faith is Faith Lived

Faith is not meant only for Sunday mornings or whenever we go to church. Faith is the lens through which every decision, every relationship, and every action is filtered. Pope Leo XIV in his sermon on August 24, 2025 said, "Faith is not separate from life." This truth means that we can't claim belief in God yet live as though He is absent from our work, our family, or our choices. People should see our faith, our Christianity, through and in our actions.

Faith lived out looks like:

- Choosing honesty when dishonesty would be easier.
- Offering forgiveness even when resentment feels justified.
- Extending love to those who seem unlovable.
- Being kind even when we feel hurt.
- Giving generously even when we feel forgotten.
- Including others when we feel excluded.

When we intentionally live faith daily, we become living testimonies of God's presence. People can see Jesus in us and through us.

How can you better live your faith?

____

____

____

____

Empower Others

We are called to lead by example. In our authority we are called to teach truths. Your authority can be personal or professional, or both. In fact, it is your personal authority that will serve as empowerment to the world. Starting within our families as a parent, sibling, etc we lay the foundation of what is right and what is wrong. In our friendships we are an example of who to be. Professionally in our authority we can lead with love and kindness. We can empower others with every word we speak and every action we take.

Daily Choices

Empowerment doesn't happen in grand moments alone; it happens in the small, daily actions we take when we say yes to God. Choosing prayer over worry, choosing trust over fear, and choosing obedience over comfort are all ways to surrender and trust in God through daily choices. It's knowing and trusting that God will provide (surrender).

Trust transforms fear into strength. Let God's presence be your shield as you step into each day with confidence. If you need to, pray for trust and ask God to lead you. Tell Him you are working on your surrender. It is important to remember that bold faith does not require perfection. It requires daily alignment with God's will, step by step. Do not be afraid to fail and do not be afraid to ask God for His help. Let trust transform your fear into strength. Let God's presence be your shield as you step into every day with confidence.

What daily choices can you make to say yes to God?

____

____

____

____

Reflection

- What is God calling you to step into right now?
- How will you rise, align, and shine in this next season?
- What bold step of faith can you take today?

Prayer

Lord, empower me to live out all I have learned. Give me courage to step forward, align with Your truth, and shine with purpose and joy. Amen.

Walking with God

Remember that God is always there for you no matter what. Invite Him into your life. Have conversations with Him. Listen to Him. Ask Him what you should do next.

Now Go!

Work through this book and go back to revisit sections when you need to. This book is intended to be a starting point to help you *Rise. Align. Shine.* To be you! Reach out for help if you need it.

As an anthem to keep you going, I invite you to listen to the song "Thrive" by Casting Crowns.
(lyrics shared here are provided by Genius.com)

Use the Bridge as a chant to remind what can be:

Joy Unspeakable, Faith Unsinkable
Love Unstoppable, Anything is possible
Joy Unspeakable, Faith Unsinkable
Love Unstoppable, Anything is possible
Joy Unspeakable, Faith Unsinkable
Love Unstoppable, Anything is possible
Joy Unspeakable, Faith Unsinkable
Love Unstoppable, Anything is possible

The chorus says it all! We were made to thrive!

Just to know You and
To make You known
We lift Your name on High
Shine like the sun make darkness run and hide
We know we were made for so much more
Than ordinary lives
It's time for us to more than just survive
We were made to thrive

Use this book to help you thrive!
Michele

About the Author

Michele Gunn is a Gallup-Certified Strengths Coach, author, and speaker dedicated to helping women discover who God created them to be. Drawing on her experience as a wife, mother, grandmother, and professional leader, Michele blends practical wisdom with faith-based guidance to inspire women to embrace their strengths, cultivate clarity, and live with confidence.

Through her coaching practice, *Cultivate and Thrive,* and her online column, *Graceful Awakening* on Patheos, Michele encourages Christian women to rise above fear, align with their God-given purpose, and shine with lasting joy. She speaks and writes on topics of faith, personal growth, and empowerment, equipping women to live authentically and leave a legacy of light.

When she's not writing or coaching, Michele enjoys time with her family and finding joy in life's simple, God-given moments.

Michele has written many magazine articles and has contributed to a few anthologies. You can find her at:

www.michelegunn.com
Amazon Author page: https://amzn.to/4o6Utqa
Graceful Awakening
(https://www.patheos.com/blogs/gracefulawakening/
LinkedIn: https://www.linkedin.com/in/michelegunn/
Facebook: https://www.facebook.com/michele.jonasgunn
Instagram: https://www.instagram.com/michelegunn1
Tiktok: https://www.tiktok.com/@michelegunn1